ENCOUNTERS WITH JESUS

ALSO BY TIMOTHY KELLER

The Reason for God: *Belief in an Age of Skepticism*

The Prodigal God: *Recovering the Heart of the
Christian Faith*

Counterfeit Gods: *The Empty Promises of Money, Sex, and
Power, and the Only Hope That Matters*

Generous Justice: *How God's Grace Makes Us Just*

Jesus the King: *Understanding the Life and Death of the Son
of God*

The Meaning of Marriage: *Facing the Complexities of
Commitment with the Wisdom of God*

Every Good Endeavor: *Connecting Your Work to God's Work*

Walking with God through Pain and Suffering

REDEEMER

ENCOUNTERS
WITH JESUS

Unexpected Answers to
Life's Biggest Questions

Timothy Keller

DUTTON

DUTTON

Published by the Penguin Group
Penguin Group (USA) LLC
375 Hudson Street
New York, New York 10014

USA | Canada | UK | Ireland | Australia | New Zealand | India | South Africa | China
penguin.com
A Penguin Random House Company

Copyright © 2013 by Timothy Keller
Penguin supports copyright. Copyright fuels creativity, encourages diverse voices, promotes
free speech, and creates a vibrant culture. Thank you for buying an authorized edition of this
book and for complying with copyright laws by not reproducing, scanning, or distributing
any part of it in any form without permission. You are supporting writers and allowing Penguin to continue to publish books for every reader.

All Bible references are from the New International Version (NIV), unless otherwise noted.

The chapters in this book were published individually
in slightly different forms as the Encounters with Jesus eSeries.

 REGISTERED TRADEMARK—MARCA REGISTRADA

LIBRARY OF CONGRESS CATALOGING-IN-PUBLICATION DATA
has been applied for.

ISBN 978-0-525-95435-4

Printed in the United States of America
1 3 5 7 9 10 8 6 4 2

Set in Galliard
Designed by Leonard Telesca

*To the ministers and staff of the campus ministries
who brought me to faith and also nurtured the faith of my sons
and their wives, in particular those working in
Reformed University Fellowship in the United States
and
Universities and Colleges Christian Fellowship,
the successor to Inter-Varsity Fellowship, in the United Kingdom.*

Contents

Contents

INTRODUCTION

I was raised in a mainline Protestant church, but in college I went through personal and spiritual crises that led me to question my most fundamental beliefs about God, the world, and myself.

During those years I fell in with some Christians who were active in small-group Bible studies. In these groups the leader would not take the role of teacher or instructor; instead he or she would facilitate the entire group's reading and interpretation of the chosen Bible text. The ground rules were simple but crucial for the integrity of the exercise. The Bible was to be given the benefit of the doubt—the text was to be treated as reliable and its authors as competent. No one person's interpretation was to be imposed on the passage; we were to come to conclusions as a group. We sought to mine the riches of the material as a community, assuming that together we would see far more than any individual could.

Before I was even sure where I stood in my own faith, I was asked to lead a group and was provided with a set of Bible studies entitled *Conversations with Jesus Christ from the Gospel of John* by Marilyn Kunz and Catherine Schell. It covered thirteen passages in the book of John where Jesus had conversations with individuals. Those studies helped my group uncover layers of meaning and insight that astonished us all. Moving through these accounts of Jesus' life, I began to sense more than ever before that the Bible was not an ordinary book. Yes, it carried the strange beauty of literature from the remote past; but there was something else. It was through these studies of encounters with Jesus that I began to sense an inexplicable life and power in the text. These conversations from centuries ago were uncannily relevant and incisive *to me—right now*. I began to search the Scriptures not just for intellectual stimulation but in order to find God.

I was taught that patience and thoughtfulness were keys to insight. At one point I went to a conference for Bible study leaders. I'll never forget one of the exercises. The instructor gave us one verse, Mark 1:17 (ESV): "And Jesus said to them, 'Follow me, and I will make you become fishers of men.'" She asked us to spend thirty minutes studying the verse (which, naturally, was taken from an encounter with Jesus). She warned us that after five or ten minutes we would think we had seen all there was to see, but she challenged us to keep going. "Write down at least thirty things you see in or learn from the verse." Ten minutes into the exercise I was finished (or so I thought) and bored. But I dutifully pushed on and kept looking. To my surprise there was more. When we all returned she asked us to look at our list and circle the most penetrating, moving, and personally helpful insight. Then she asked us a question: "How many of you discovered your best insight in the first five minutes? Raise your hands." No hands. "How many after ten minutes?" One or two hands. "Fifteen?" More. "Twenty?" A large number now raised their hands. "Twenty-five?" Many of us now raised our hands, smiling and shaking our heads.

Those initial experiences with patient, inductive study of the biblical text changed my spiritual life. I discovered that if I spent the time and assumed the proper attitude of openness and trust, God spoke to me through his Word. They also set me on my vocational course by giving me the tools to help other people hear God's Word through the Bible. For nearly forty years I've been teaching and preaching the Bible for people, but the basis for every talk, lecture, or sermon has always been what I learned in college about how to sit with a text and carefully plumb its depths.

I still accept the authority of all of the Bible, and love learning and teaching from all of it. But I first felt the personal weight of the Bible's spiritual authority in the Gospels, particularly in those conversations Jesus had with individuals—the skeptical student Nathanael, Jesus' bewildered mother at the wedding feast, the religion professor who came at night, the woman at the well, the bereaved sisters Mary and Martha, and many others.

I suppose you could say that many of my own formative encounters with Jesus came from studying his encounters with individuals in the Gospels.

SEVERAL YEARS AGO, I wrote a book called *The Reason for God: Belief in an Age of Skepticism.* As a pastor in New York City for many years, I've always appreciated skeptics' arguments and the invaluable role they play in defining and clarifying what is unique about Christianity. It bothers me when Christians dismiss these questions glibly or condescendingly. I remember very clearly the doubts and questions I brought to those Bible study groups back in college and how grateful I was to have them taken seriously. I've seen that taking the time and effort to answer hard questions gives believers the opportunity to deepen their own faith while creating the possibility that doubtful people may become open to the joy of Christianity.

So I was delighted to be asked to speak for five nights to students—most of them skeptics—in Oxford Town Hall in Oxford, England, in 2012. We agreed that I would explore encounters that individuals had with Jesus Christ in the Gospel of John. I felt this was a good choice for the setting because the accounts of these encounters reveal the core teachings and personality of Jesus in a particularly compelling way, as I had discovered personally so many years before. As I prepared to give the talks, it struck me that these encounters were apropos for another reason. In many of them we see Jesus addressing the big, universal, "meaning of life" questions: What is the world for? What's wrong with it? What (if anything) can make it right, and how? How can we be a part of making it right? And where should we look for answers to these questions in the first place? These were the big questions that everyone must ask—and that honest skeptics are particularly keen to explore.

Everyone has a working theory about the answers to these questions. If you try to live without them, you will soon be overwhelmed by how meaningless life seems. We live at a time when some insist that we don't need any such answers, that we should admit that life is just meaningless busywork in the grand scheme of the universe and leave it at that. While you are alive, they say, just try to enjoy yourself as much as you can, and when you are dead, you won't be around to worry about it. So why bother trying to find the meaning of life?

However, the French philosopher Luc Ferry (who, by the way, is in no way a Christian himself), in his book *A Brief History of Thought,* says that such statements are "too brutal to be honest." He means that people who make them cannot really believe them all the way down in their hearts. People cannot live without any hope or meaning or without a conviction that some things are more worth doing with our lives than others. And so we know we *do* have to have answers to these big questions in order, as Ferry puts it, "to live well and therefore freely, capable of joy, generosity, and love."

Ferry goes on to argue that almost all our possible answers to those big philosophical issues come from five or six major systems of thought. And today so many of the most common answers come from one system in particular. For example: Do you think it's generally a good idea to be kind to your enemies and reach out to them rather than kill them? Ferry says this idea—that you should love your enemies—came from Christianity and nowhere else. And as we will see, there are plenty of other ideas we would consider valid, or noble, or even beautiful, that came solely from Christianity.

Therefore, if you want to be sure that you are developing sound, thoughtful answers to the fundamental questions, you need at the very least to become acquainted with the teachings of Christianity. The best way to do that is to see how Jesus explained himself and his purposes to people he met—and how their lives were changed by his answers to their questions. That was the premise of the Oxford talks, which became the basis for the first five chapters of this book.

Yet I had to continue on, because once you have studied these accounts of life-changing encounters with Jesus in the flesh, and have seen the beauty of his character and his purpose, and have heard his answers to the big questions, you are still left with another question: How can *I* encounter Jesus all these centuries later? Can I be changed just as these eyewitnesses were changed?

The Christian gospel says that we are saved—changed forever—not by what we do, and not even by what Jesus says to people he meets, but by what he has done for us. And so we can best discover the life-changing grace and power of Jesus if we look at what he has accomplished in the main events of his life: his birth, his sufferings in the wilderness and the garden of Gethsemane, his last hours with the disciples, his death on the cross, and his resurrection and ascension. It is through his actions in these moments that Jesus accomplishes a salvation in our place that we could never have achieved ourselves. Seeing this can move you from an acquaintance with Jesus as a teacher and historical figure to a life-changing encounter with him as redeemer and savior.

So the second half of the book will look at some of these pivotal events in Jesus' life. The basis for these chapters was a series of talks I gave at the Harvard Club of New York City, where I spoke at regular breakfast meetings to business, government, and cultural leaders over a period of several years. As with the Oxford talks, many of those in the room were highly educated and accomplished people who helpfully shared their own doubts and questions with me. And in both sets of talks, I was going back—as I have again and again through the decades—to these Gospel texts where I first felt the "alive and active" character of the Scriptures (Hebrews 4:12). Just as my instructor had taught me, every time I discovered more and more within them, and every time I was more excited to share what I had learned.

There is one more reason I wanted to write this book. When my granddaughter Lucy was eighteen months old, it was clear that she could perceive far more than she could express. She would point at something or pick up something and then stare at me in deep frustration. She wanted to communicate something, but she was too young to do it. All people feel this kind of frustration at various points throughout their lives. You experience something profound and then you come down off the mountaintop or out of the concert hall or wherever you were and you try to convey it to somebody else. But your words can't begin to do it justice.

Certainly all Christians will feel like that when they want to describe their experiences of God. As a teacher and preacher, it is my job and greatest desire to help other people see the sheer beauty of who Christ is and what he has done. But the inadequacy of my words (or perhaps any words) to fully convey this beauty is a constant frustration and grief to me. Yet there is no place in the world that helps us more in this difficult project than these accounts of Jesus' encounters with people in the Gospels.

I hope that whether you are looking at these accounts for the first time or the hundredth, you will be struck again by the person of Christ and what he has done for us.

ENCOUNTERS WITH JESUS

ONE

THE SKEPTICAL STUDENT

The first encounter I want to look at is a subtle but power-ful one with a skeptical student. It addresses perhaps the most fundamental of all the big questions of life: Where should we look for answers to the big questions of life? And where *shouldn't* we look for answers? So it speaks to those who are skeptical about Christianity, and also to Christians who face skepticism from those who do not believe.

This encounter comes just after what has been called the Prologue at the beginning of the book of John. Luc Ferry, the French philosopher, points out that this prologue was one of the turning points in the history of thought. The Greeks be-lieved that the universe had a rational and moral order to it, and this "order of nature" they called the *Logos*. For the Greeks the meaning of life was to contemplate and discern this order in the world, and they defined a well-lived life as one that conformed to it. The Gospel writer John deliberately borrows the Greek philosophical term *Logos* and says this about Jesus:

> In the beginning was the word (*Logos*), and the word was with God, and the word was God. He was with God in the beginning. Through Him, all things were made. Without Him, nothing was made that has been made. In Him was life, and in that life was the light of all mankind. . . . And the word became flesh, and dwelt among us, and we beheld his glory. (John 1:1–3, 14)

This statement fell like a thunderbolt onto the world of the ancient philosophers. Like the Greek philosophers, and unlike many contemporary ones, John affirms that there is a *telos*, or purpose, to our lives—something we were made for, that we must recognize and honor in order to live well and freely. He proclaims that the world is not just the product of blind, random forces; its history is not "a tale told by an idiot, full of sound and fury, signifying nothing." But then the Bible goes on to insist that the meaning of life is not a principle or some other abstract rational structure, but a *person*, an individual human being who walked the earth. As Ferry notes, this claim struck philosophers as "insanity." But it led to a revolution. If Christianity was true, a well-lived life was not found primarily in philosophical contemplation and intellectual pursuits, which would leave out most of the people of the world. Rather, it was found in a person to be encountered in a relationship that could be available to anyone, anywhere, from any background.

To show us immediately how this works in real life, John brings it down to earth by showing Jesus interacting with a group of students. Back in the days of Jesus there were no universities; if you wanted to be a student, you attached yourself to a teacher. There were a lot of spiritual teachers, and many followed them and became their students, or disciples. Perhaps the edgiest and most avant-garde teacher of that time was John the Baptist. He was very popular, with many followers and a number of dedicated students. History has recorded some of them: Andrew, who had a brother, Peter; and Philip, who brought his friend Nathanael. Some of the students already believed what their teacher was saying about the coming Messiah, the one John called "the lamb of God" (John 1:29). But a few of them were skeptical. Nathanael was one of these skeptical students, until he had an encounter with Jesus Christ:

> The next day Jesus decided to leave for Galilee. Finding Philip, he said to him, "Follow me." Philip, like Andrew and Peter, was from the town of Bethsaida. Philip found Nathanael and told him, "We have found the one Moses wrote about in the Law, and about whom the prophets also wrote—Jesus of Nazareth, the son of Joseph." "Nazareth! Can any-

thing good come from there?" Nathanael asked. "Come and see," said Philip. When Jesus saw Nathanael approaching, he said of him, "Here is a true Israelite, in whom there is nothing false." "How do you know me?" Nathanael asked. Jesus answered, "I saw you while you were still under the fig tree before Philip called you." Then Nathanael declared, "Rabbi, you are the Son of God; you are the King of Israel." Jesus said, "You believe because I told you I saw you under the fig tree. You will see greater things than that." He then added, "I tell you the truth, you shall see Heaven open, and the angels of God ascending and descending on the Son of Man." (John 1:43–51)

First, I want you to notice Nathanael's problem. Nathanael is at least an intellectual snob, and maybe even a bigot. Philip comes to him and says, "I want you to meet this new rabbi, he's got answers to the big questions of our time, and he's from Nazareth." Nathanael sneers, "Nazareth!?" Everybody from Jerusalem looked down on people from Galilee. This kind of attitude is characteristic of the human race. Some neighborhoods have always looked down at other neighborhoods as being "the wrong side of the tracks." And how do people who are looked down upon deal with it? They go looking for other people on whom *they* can look down. And so it goes endlessly. Though Nathanael was not from Jerusalem but from one part of Galilee, he felt he could look down on a place like Nazareth, which was considered to be in an even more backwater and primitive region of Galilee. Always there are the right people, there are the suitable people, there are the smart people, and then there are (lower your voice) *those others.* And the way you signal to other right, smart, and suitable people that you are one of them is to roll your eyes when the wrong people and places are mentioned.

We want others to think of us as capable and intelligent, and we often seek to establish this identity not through respectful, diligent argument but through ridicule and disdain. People are not merely mistaken but out of step, regressive, intellectual midgets. Nathanael could not believe that somebody from a place like Nazareth had the answers to the big questions of our time. "You're telling me he's got the answers— and he's from Nazareth? Uh, I don't think so." He's rolling his eyes. "He's from *there? Really?*"

If you have this view of Christianity, or know someone who has this view of Christianity, that is no surprise. Many people today view Christianity much like Nathanael viewed Nazareth. Christianity was from Nazareth then, and it is still from Nazareth today. People love to roll their eyes at their idea of Christianity and its claims about who Christ is and what he has done and can do for them. The knowing people, the suitable people, all say, "Christianity—been there, done that. I grew up with it,

I realized early on it's not for me, and I've made up my mind." So Jesus is still from Nazareth.

If that is your attitude toward Christianity, I have two suggestions for you, because I think you have two issues before you. The first is that this kind of dismissiveness is always deadly. It absolutely kills all creativity and problem solving, not to mention any hope of a relationship. Tara Parker-Pope, in her book on marriage called *For Better*, cites eye-rolling as one of the definitive warning signs that a relationship is in serious trouble. Marriage counselors look out for it because it signals contempt for the other person. A successful marriage can handle disappointment, disagreement, pain, and frustration. But it can't handle complete dismissal of the other; contempt literally kills the relationship. A more concrete example is one where you have misplaced your keys. Once you've looked for them in all the places where they "can" be and haven't found them, you'll have to start looking in places where they "can't" be. And of course, that's where you'll find them. So there's nothing more fatal to wisdom and good relationships than rejecting certain ideas—or certain people—out of hand.

Your second issue is more substantial. By despising Christianity, you sever the living taproot to what are probably many of your own core values. As we noted, Christianity originated one of the foundational ideas of peaceful civilization—that you should love your enemies, not kill them. Another idea foundational to our contemporary consciousness, as Luc Ferry points out, is the concept that every single human being, regardless of talent or wealth or race or gender, is made in God's personal image and therefore has dignity and rights. Ferry says that without Christianity's teaching that the *Logos* is a person, "the philosophy of human rights to which we subscribe today would never have established itself."

Another view, taken for granted today, that came from the Bible, is that you should take care of the poor. In pre-Christian Europe, when the monks were propagating Christianity, all of the elites thought that loving your enemies and taking care of the poor was crazy. They said society would fall apart, because that's not the way the world works. The talented and the strong prevail. The winner takes all. The strong prey on the weak. The poor are born to suffer. Isn't that how everything's always worked? But the teachings of Christianity revolutionized pagan Europe by stressing the dignity of the person, the primacy of love, including toward enemies, and the care of the poor and orphans.

You may say, "Well, that's an interesting historical argument, that these ideas came from the Bible and the church. But I can believe in them without believing in Christianity." That may be true at one level; but I'd like you to see that it's a shortsighted response.

The book of Genesis is a window into what cultures were like before the revelation of the Bible. One thing we see early on is the widespread practice of primogeniture—the eldest son inherited all the wealth, which is how they ensured the family kept its status and place in society. So the second or third son got nothing, or very little. Yet all through the Bible, when God chooses someone to work through, he chooses the younger sibling. He chooses Abel over Cain. He chooses Isaac over Ishmael. He chooses Jacob over Esau. He chooses David over all *eleven* of his older brothers. Time after time he chooses not the oldest, not the one the world expects and rewards. Never the one from Jerusalem, as it were, but always the one from Nazareth.

Another ancient cultural tradition revealed in Genesis is that in those societies, women who had lots of children were extolled as heroic. If you had many children, that meant economic success, it meant military success, and of course it meant the odds of carrying on the family name were secure. So women who could not have children were shamed and stigmatized. Yet throughout the Bible, when God shows us how he works through a woman, he chooses the ones who cannot have children, and opens their wombs. These are despised women, but God chooses them over ones who are loved and blessed in the eyes of the world. He chooses Sarah, Abraham's wife; Rebecca, Isaac's wife; Samuel's mother, Hannah; and John's mother, Elizabeth. God always works through the men or the boys nobody wanted, through the women or girls nobody wanted.

You might be thinking how nice and uplifting this part of

Christianity is—God loves underdogs. You might say to yourself, "I can agree with that part of the Bible. But all the other parts about the wrath of God and the blood of Christ and the resurrection of the body, I don't accept." But those parts of the Bible—the challenging, supernatural parts—are central, not peripheral. The heart of the unique message of the Bible is that the transcendent, immortal God came to earth himself and became weak, vulnerable to suffering and death. He did this all for us—all to atone for our sin, to take the punishment we deserved. If it is true, it is the most astonishing and radical act of self-giving and loving sacrifice that can be imagined. There could be no stronger basis and dynamic motivation for the revolutionary Christian ethical concepts that attract us. What made Christian ethics unique was not that Jesus and the early Christians were such nice people doing all these nice things to make the world a nice place to live. These ideas never made sense to anyone until people came to understand the Christian message about the nature of ultimate reality—and that message is summarized in what the Bible calls "the gospel."

The essence of what makes Christianity different from every other religion and form of thought is this: Every other religion says if you want to find God, if you want to improve yourself, if you want to have higher consciousness, if you want to connect with the divine, however it is defined—you have to *do* something. You have to gather your strength, you have to keep the rules, you have to free your mind, then you have to fill your mind, and you have to be above average. Every other religion or human philosophy says if you want to make the world right, or make yourself right, then summon all your reason and your strength, and live in a certain way.

Christianity says the exact opposite. Every other religion and philosophy says you have to do something to connect to God; but Christianity says no, Jesus Christ came to do for you what you couldn't do for yourself. Every other religion says here are the answers to the big questions, but Christianity says Jesus *is* the answer to them all. So many systems of thought appeal to strong, successful people, because they play directly into their belief that if you are strong and hardworking enough, you will prevail. But Christianity is not just for the strong; it's for everyone, especially for people who admit that, where it really counts, they're weak. It is for people who have the particular kind of strength to admit that their flaws are not superficial, their heart is deeply disordered, and that they are incapable of rectifying themselves. It is for those who can see that they need a savior, that they need Jesus Christ dying on the cross, to put them right with God.

Think about what I've just written. It sounds counterintuitive at best and off-putting at worst. The very genius of Christianity is that it's *not* about "Here's what you have to do to find God." Christianity is about God coming to earth in the form of Jesus Christ, dying on the cross, to find you. *That* is the truly radical and unique truth that Christianity has contributed to the world. All the other revolutionary ideas about caring for the weak and needy, living for love and service instead of power and success, loving even your enemies sacrificially—all flow from the gospel itself; namely, that because of the depth of our sin, God came in the person of Jesus Christ to do what we could not do for ourselves, to save us.

Now I ask you—if you concede the source of many of your convictions, why embrace one part of the Christian teaching without accepting the other part that explains it and makes it coherent? Do not be like Nathanael. Do not let a conviction that Christianity is simply outdated or intellectually unsophisticated blind you to what it offers. Watch out for your pride and your prejudice. Be aware of contempt and dismissiveness. It is toxic in all aspects of life, but especially here at the point of asking the foundational questions.

So the first important aspect of Nathanael's story is the problem of pride and contempt. But beyond that, despite his scoffing, he has a deep underlying spiritual need. He says, "Nazareth! Can anything good come from there?" and yet only a few moments later he is saying, "Rabbi, you are the Son of God; you are the King of Israel." Once Jesus begins to give him some credible evidence for who he is, Nathanael shifts allegiances very quickly—probably too quickly. (As we will see later, Jesus mildly rebukes Nathanael for not taking time to think it out.) Does this surprise you? It doesn't surprise me.

When my wife, Kathy, and I moved to Manhattan more

than twenty years ago, we wanted to start a new church. We were told that New York City was filled with the young, the ambitious, and the brilliant, and that if you started a church in Manhattan, nobody would come because they all think they know better. They looked down on organized religion, we were told, and especially Christianity. Christianity, remember, is from Nazareth. They rolled their eyes at it. So nobody's going to come. But curiously, that did not happen; today, Redeemer has more than five thousand people who regularly attend Sunday service. It is a thriving community.

The reason for all this is the same reason Nathanael changed. Underneath the loud, public assertions of skepticism there was a lot of covert spiritual searching going on. All those young, ambitious, and brilliant people wanted to *look* like they didn't care too much about answering the foundational questions or that they had found them in whatever they were furiously pursuing. But underneath, they had the same need we all have, and that none of us can escape. They had to look for answers. And many found them in Christianity.

In the same way, despite all his bluster, notice that Nathanael nonetheless went with Philip to meet Jesus. Why did he do it? Like many young Jews in his generation, Nathanael was struggling with the fact that the Jews were under the boot of Rome, and they had no idea what God was doing. They were having a collective racial identity crisis. Should they be looking for a messiah? What was their future? Were they still

God's people or not? Had God rejected them? Evidently he wasn't satisfied with the answers to these questions he got from others. He must not have been very happy with his own understanding of things and, perhaps, with his own spiritual condition. So he thought, "Maybe I should look at Nazareth, as unbelievable as that sounds."

Students today wrestle with different forms of the big questions in life, but many of them are also unsatisfied with the answers they have gotten in the most respected schools and books and may, like Nathanael, quietly begin to investigate Jesus. A classic example of this move occurred in the life of the famous poet, W. H. Auden, who moved to Manhattan in 1939. By that time he was already a great writer, and he had abandoned his childhood faith in the Church of England, as had most of his friends in the British intellectual classes. But after World War II broke out, he changed his mind, and he embraced the truth of Christianity and shocked many by going back to the church.

What happened? In his account of his spiritual renewal he observed that the novelty and shock of the Nazis in the 1940s was that they made no pretense of believing in justice and liberty for all—they attacked Christianity on the grounds that "to love one's neighbor as oneself was a command fit only for effeminate weaklings."[1] Moreover, "the utter denial of everything liberalism had ever stood for was arousing wild enthusiasm not in some barbaric land, but in one of the most highly educated countries in Europe." In light of all this, Auden did not believe that he could any longer assume that the values of liberalism (by which he meant freedom, reason, democracy, and human dignity) were self-evident.

> If I am convinced that the highly educated Nazis are wrong, and that we highly educated English are right, what is it that validates our values and invalidates theirs? The English intellectuals who now cry to Heaven against the evil incarnated in Hitler have no Heaven to cry to. The whole trend of liberal thought has been to undermine faith in the absolute. It has tried to make reason the judge. But since life is a changing process the attempt to find human space for keeping a promise leads to the inevitable conclusion that I can break it whenever I feel it convenient. Either we serve the Unconditional, or some Hitlerian monster will supply an iron convention to do evil by.

Christianity—even for Auden, who was raised in the church—was from Nazareth. He had moved away from it as obsolete and unhelpful. But the rise of the Nazis made him see something. He believed in human rights, in liberty and freedom. But why did he? The operational principle of the natural world is that the strong eat the weak. So if it's natural for the strong to eat the weak, and if we just got here only through the natural, unguided process of evolution, why do we suddenly turn around when the strong nations start to eat the weak nations and say, *That is wrong?* On what basis can we do that? On what basis can we say that genocide in the Sudan, where a strong ethnic group "eats" the weak one, is wrong? If there is no God, then my views of justice are just my opinion—so how then can we denounce the Nazis?

Auden realized that unless there was a God, he had no right to tell anybody else that his feelings or ideas were more valid than their feelings or ideas. He saw that unless there was a God, all the values we cherish are imaginary. And because he was sure they were *not* imaginary—that genocide was indeed absolutely wrong—he concluded that there must be a God.

Like the skeptical student Nathanael, Auden was haunted by the fact that the "right people" of his time laughed at Christianity. But his unanswered intellectual questions—about the grounding of moral values, among other matters—made him willing to look at Jesus anew. And he had the same experience that Nathanael did when he opened himself to the man from Nazareth. He believed.

In Alasdair MacIntyre's book *After Virtue*, the philosopher offers the kind of reasoning that brought the poet Auden to faith. MacIntyre argues that you can never determine whether something is good or bad unless you know its *telos*. So he asks, for example, how can you tell whether a watch is a good one or a bad one? You have to know what its purpose is. If I try to hammer a nail with my watch, and it breaks, should I complain that it is a "bad watch"? Of course not; it wasn't made to hammer nails. That is not its purpose. Its purpose is to tell you the time at a glance. The same principle should apply to humanity. How can you say that someone is a good person or a bad person unless you know what they are designed for, what their purpose is?

Ah, but wait. What if you say, "I don't know if there is a God or not, and I don't think human beings were designed for anything." Do you see your dilemma now? If you believe that, you should never speak about good or bad people again. If you believe we have no design or purpose, and you still say about some people, "They are not living right—they are doing wrong," then you are being inconsistent or disingenuous.

I cannot prove that Christianity is true. But I can show you there are sound reasons to believe in Jesus. If you, like Nathanael, are willing to admit the depth of your need to discover better answers to the big questions than you are getting, and if you are willing to stop rolling your eyes at Christianity, I invite you to consider the man who came from Nazareth. Considering the world-changing ideas that have come from there, there is no good reason not to.

The third aspect of Nathanael's story to examine is the prescription Jesus gives him to meet his need. Jesus says two things to Nathanael when he meets him.

First he refers to him as an Israelite "in whom there is nothing false." For Jesus to say that Nathanael was a transparent, straight-talking person was probably putting it rather nicely. Others might have characterized Nathanael as abrasive. Probably a lot of people didn't like him because he was so outspoken and was always stepping on people's toes. But Jesus shows us something about himself here. He can see us to the bottom but is nonetheless gentle with us. Nathanael is surprised at his insight (and maybe his generosity of spirit) and asks, "How do you know me so well?"

And then Jesus slips in, "I saw you under the fig tree." Now, parenthetically, one of the reasons we can trust that this is an eyewitness account is that nowhere else are we ever told what was happening under the fig tree or why it was significant. And if you're making up a fictional story, you don't do that, because it doesn't move the plot forward and raises distracting issues for readers. So what was Nathanael doing under the fig tree? Nobody knows. All that matters is that Nathanael couldn't believe that Jesus knew about it. It was so private, so significant, so astounding to him that Jesus would know that and still affirm him. He says, "You are the king of Israel! You are the Messiah!"

And Jesus gently rebukes him. He says, "Oh, first you were too skeptical, and now you're ready to adopt me; but I haven't even begun to talk to you about who I really am. Yesterday you were rolling your eyes, and today you've had an emotional experience. You've found a man who has supernatural knowledge of you. But slow down; don't be so impressed by appearances. You really still don't understand who I am."

Jesus' disciple Thomas, after the resurrection, tells the other disciples, "I'm not going to believe that he was raised from the dead until I see the nail prints in his hands and put my finger in them." When Jesus then appears to Thomas he does not say, "How dare you question me?" He says, "Here, look. Now stop doubting and start believing." In other words, Jesus says, "I like the fact that you expect to get reasons to believe in me, and I'll give you reasons because you're looking for them in good faith." Jesus is not against people thinking. In fact he's insisting that Nathanael do a little *more* thinking.

And therefore, if you're skeptical about Christianity, I would like you to realize that you have a balance to strike. First, to remain skeptical forever is intellectually and morally self-defeating. On the other hand, surrendering to the first idea that you hope will solve your deep emotional needs will not answer any questions for you in the end. It's not enough to turn to Christianity simply because it meets some perceived needs. Christianity is not a consumer good. You should turn to it only if it is *true*.

Did you notice the last thing Jesus says to Nathanael? He says, "You believe because of that? I tell you the truth, you shall see angels of God ascending and descending on the Son of Man." See, when you first come to Jesus you think, I'm probably not going to get answers to the big questions, but maybe he'll help me be a better person; maybe he'll deal with my loneliness or some other problem. You always come to Jesus hedging your bets, staying guarded as to whether you'll get your needs met.

But when you actually find him, he'll always be far more than you ever imagined him to be. When he says that Nathanael will see angels ascending and descending on the son of man, he's referring to the time in the Old Testament where Jacob falls asleep and sees a ladder between Earth and Heaven, and angels ascending and descending on the ladder. Angels are a sign of the royal presence of God. Because people have turned from God and have destroyed one another, there's a slab, as it were, between Heaven and Earth. A wall between the ideal and the real. But Jacob has this vision, this dream that somehow, someday there will be a connection between Heaven and Earth, and there will be some way to get into the very presence of God. And here Jesus makes the incredible claim that he *is* that way. He is the *Logos* of the universe, the bridge between Heaven and Earth.

You can almost hear Jesus laugh as he responds to Nathanael. He says, in effect, "Oh my! You think I'm the Messiah. You probably think I'm going to get on a horse and throw down the Roman oppressors. But I'm going to show you far greater things than that. Doing that would not change the whole human condition, defeat evil and death, and renew the world. I tell you, I am the *axis mundi*. I have punched a hole in the slab between Heaven and Earth. Through my incarnation as a human being, and through my death on the cross, which you haven't even seen yet, I can bring you right into the presence of God."

Though most spiritual seekers start their search afraid of disappointment, Jesus says that he will always be infinitely more than anyone is looking for. He will always exceed our expectations; he will be more than we can ask for or imagine.

So shed your prejudices and come look along with Nathanael. Come look and talk about Jesus with your friends. Come and be ready to have your priorities and categories changed. Whatever you are expecting, whatever you are hoping, whatever you are dreaming—you will discover something much greater in Nazareth.

TWO

The Insider and the Outcast

In the stories of the Insider and the Outcast, we will specifically ask, What is wrong with the world the way it is? Because we can't move on to talking about what we should do to make the world better unless we understand clearly what is wrong with it. Diagnosis comes before prescription. And I believe we will find a sound set of answers here.

In the third chapter of the Gospel of John, Jesus Christ meets a highly moral insider, a leader in the civic and religious establishment; in the following chapter, he meets a social, moral, and religious outsider—an outcast—who happens to be a woman. Both texts are well known to many Christians because they develop their characters in some detail and are full of memorable dialogue. It is interesting, though, that whenever anyone teaches about these texts they almost always treat either one or the other, never both together. But I think that is a mistake. I believe there is a reason these two encounters appear one after the other in this Gospel: The writer wants us to consider them together. These two persons appear on the surface to be so different, and their circumstances so dissimilar, that at first glance it seems they could not have anything to do with each other. But the author is leading us to ask: As different as the Insider and the Outcast are, what do they have in common? Because if these two people have something in common, then we *all* have something in common. So looking at these encounters together will help us see what John is saying about the state of the world and the role we all play in making the world what it is today.

There is no way to talk about these encounters without addressing the subject of sin. I know the words *sin* and *sinner* carry a lot of cultural baggage, and I can understand why people cringe when they hear a Christian use them. The words have unfortunately been used to marginalize and objectify those who are not Christians. It's easy to say, "You're not only someone who disagrees with me, you're a *sinner*." It's a word that has been used to climb up to a false high moral ground and cast judgment on those below. If you are a sinner (but, by implication, I am not) then instead of having an actual discussion and placing myself genuinely in the path of your questions, I marginalize you.

Obviously, I believe this understanding of sin is wrong. The proper biblical understanding of sin is much more radical and far-reaching. It can never be used as a weapon, because it will recoil on anyone who tries to deploy it that way. Biblically, *no one* can escape the verdict of being a sinner. And that is the point of these two stories.

Let's first address the Outcast's encounter with Jesus, because it starts us off with a picture of sin that most people would recognize. This encounter with a woman at a well is found in John 4. Jesus is traveling with his disciples through Samaria, which is outside of Judea. When he gets to the town, his disciples leave to get something to eat. Jesus is very weary and thirsty. And at the sixth hour, which is noon, in the heat of the day, he goes to a well. He has no way of getting water out of the well because he does not have a water jar. But then a solitary woman comes to draw water from the well, and he says,

> "Will you give me a drink?"
>
> The Samaritan woman says to him, "You are a Jew and I am a Samaritan woman. How can you ask me for a drink?" [For Jews do not associate with Samaritans.]
>
> Jesus answered her, "If you knew the gift of God and who it is that asks you for a drink, you would have asked him and he would have given you living water."
>
> "Sir," the woman said, "you have nothing to draw with and the well is deep. Where can you get

this living water? Are you greater than our father Jacob, who gave us the well and drank from it himself, as did also his sons and his livestock?"

Jesus answered, "Everyone who drinks this water will be thirsty again, but whoever drinks the water I give them will never thirst. Indeed, the water I give them will become in them a spring of water welling up to eternal life."

The woman said to him, "Sir, give me this water so that I won't get thirsty and have to keep coming here to draw water."

He told her, "Go, call your husband and come back."

"I have no husband," she replied.

Jesus said to her, "You are right when you say you have no husband. The fact is, you have had five husbands, and the man you now have is not your husband. What you have just said is quite true."

"Sir," the woman said, "I can see that you are a prophet" (John 4:7–19).

Before we continue with the encounter, let me show you what a remarkable conversation this already is.

The first striking feature of this story is the radical move Jesus makes by initiating a conversation. It doesn't seem unusual to us to see these two talking, but it should. Notice her shock that he is even speaking to her, for the Jews and Samaritans were bitter enemies. Centuries before, most of the Jews were exiled to Babylon by their conquerors. Some of the Jews who stayed behind intermarried with other Canaanites and essentially formed a new tribe, the Samaritans. They took parts of the Jewish religion and parts of the Canaanite religion and created a syncretistic religion. So the Jews considered the Samaritans racially inferior *and* heretics. That's the first reason she is surprised he is even speaking to her. But on top of that, it was scandalous for a Jewish man to speak to any strange woman in public.

What's more, she had come to draw water at noon. Many biblical scholars have pointed out that this is not when women ordinarily came to draw water. They came early in the day when it wasn't hot yet, so they could have water for the housekeeping chores for the entire day. So why was she there alone, in the middle of the day? The answer is, she was a moral outcast, a complete outsider—even within her own marginalized part of society.

And so when Jesus begins to speak to her, he is deliberately reaching across almost every significant barrier that people can put up between themselves. In this case, a racial barrier, a cultural barrier, a gender barrier, and a moral barrier—and every convention of the time—that he, a religious Jewish male, should have nothing whatsoever to do with her. But he doesn't care. Do you see how radical that is? He reaches right across all the human divides in order to connect to her. She is amazed, and we should be amazed, too.

The second interesting feature about this encounter is that, though he is clearly open and warm to her, he still confronts her. But he does so in a gentle and artful way. He begins by saying, "If you knew who I was, you would ask me for *living* water; and if you drink that water you will never thirst again."

What on earth is Jesus talking about? He is speaking metaphorically, referring to "living water," which he calls "eternal life." The image is a little lost on us. Almost everywhere in the United States today we have ready access to drinking water. Most of us know very little about real thirst, but those who lived in an arid climate next to a desert knew a lot about it. Because our bodies contain so much water, to be in profound thirst is to be in agony. And then to taste water after you have been truly thirsty is about the most satisfying experience possible.

So what is Jesus saying to this outcast? He's saying this: "I've got something for you that is as basic and necessary to you *spiritually* as water is to you *physically*. Something without which you are absolutely lost."

But the metaphor of the living water means even more than that. Jesus is not just telling us that what he has to offer is lifesaving—he's also revealing that it satisfies from the *inside*. He says, "My water, if you get it, will become in you a spring of water welling up to eternal life." He's talking about deep soul satisfaction, about incredible satisfaction and contentment that doesn't depend on what is happening outside of us. So I ask you, what will make you happy? What will really give you a satisfying life? Almost always you will answer by thinking of something outside of you. Some of us have our hopes set on romantic love, some on career, some on politics or a social cause, and some of us on money and what it will do for us. But whatever it is that makes you say, "If I have that, if I get there, then I'll know I'm important, then I'll know I have significance, then I know I'll have security"—it's likely something outside of you. Yet Jesus says there's nothing outside of you that can truly satisfy the thirst that is deep down inside you. To continue the metaphor a bit further, you don't need water splashed on your face; you need water that comes from even deeper down inside you than the thirst itself. And Jesus is saying, "I can give it. I can put it into you. I can give you absolute, unfathomable satisfaction in the core of your being regardless of what happens outside, regardless of circumstance."

Something gets in the way of our hearing what Jesus is talking about, and I think it's that most of us aren't able to recognize our soul thirst for what it is. As long as you think there is a pretty good chance that you will achieve some of your dreams, as long as you think you have a shot at success, you experience your inner emptiness as "drive" and your anxiety as "hope." And so you can remain almost completely oblivious to how deep your thirst actually is. Most of us tell ourselves that the reason we remain unfulfilled is because we simply haven't been able to achieve our goals. And so we can live almost our entire lives without admitting to ourselves the depth of our spiritual thirst.

And that is why the few people in life who actually do reach or exceed their dreams are shocked to discover that these longed-for circumstances do not satisfy. Indeed they can enhance the inner emptiness by their presence. For example, years ago, the great tennis champion Boris Becker said, "I had won Wimbledon twice, once as the youngest player. I was rich. . . . I had all the material possessions I needed. . . . It is the old song of movie stars and pop stars who commit suicide. They have everything, and yet they are so unhappy. But I had no inner peace."[2] We might say, "I'd rather have his problem than mine." But his point is that he *has* the same problem as ours, and like us, he thought money, sex, accomplishment, and fame would solve it. The difference is, he got all those things, and in the end they didn't satisfy his thirst in the slightest. There is a famous Sophia Loren interview in which she said she had had everything—awards, marriage—but that "in my life there is an emptiness that is impossible to fulfill."[3]

Everybody has got to live for something, but Jesus is arguing that, if *he* is not that thing, it will fail you. First, it will enslave you. Whatever that thing is, you will tell yourself that you *have* to have it or there is no tomorrow. That means that if anything threatens it, you will become inordinately scared; if anyone blocks it, you will become inordinately angry; and if you fail to achieve it, you will never be able to forgive yourself. But second, if you *do* achieve it, it will fail to deliver the fulfillment you expected.

Let me give you an eloquent contemporary expression of what Jesus is saying. Nobody put this better than the American writer David Foster Wallace. He got to the top of his profession. He was an award-winning, bestselling postmodern novelist known around the world for his boundary-pushing storytelling. He once wrote a sentence that was more than a thousand words long. A few years before the end of his life, he gave a now-famous commencement speech at Kenyon College. He said to the graduating class,

> Everybody worships. The only choice we get is what to worship. And the compelling reason for maybe choosing some sort of god . . . to worship . . . is that pretty much anything else you worship will eat you alive. If you worship money and things, if they are where you tap real meaning in life, then you will never have enough, never feel you have enough. It's the truth. Worship your own body and beauty and sexual allure, and you will always feel ugly. And when time and age start showing, you will die a million deaths before [your loved ones] finally plant you. . . . Worship power, and you will end up feeling weak

and afraid, and you will need ever more power over others to numb you to your own fear. Worship your intellect, being seen as smart, you will end up feeling stupid, a fraud, always on the verge of being found out. Look, the insidious thing about these forms of worship is not that they are evil or sinful; it is that they're unconscious. They are default settings.[4]

Wallace was by no means a religious person, but he understood that everyone worships, everyone trusts in something for their salvation, everyone bases their lives on something that requires faith. A couple of years after giving that speech, Wallace killed himself. And this nonreligious man's parting words to us are pretty terrifying: "Something will eat you alive." Because even though you might never call it worship, you can be absolutely sure you are worshipping and you are seeking. And Jesus says, "Unless you're worshipping me, unless I'm the center of your life, unless you're trying to get your spiritual thirst quenched through me and not through these other things, unless you see that the solution must come inside rather than just pass by outside, then whatever you worship will abandon you in the end."

I said we often forget how thirsty we are because we believe we will fulfill our dreams. And when that happens, it's easy to walk past Jesus. But this woman at the well has no such illusions; and so the hook is set. She immediately says to Jesus,

"What is this living water? Would you give it to me?" And then he turns the tables on her and says, "Go get your husband." She replies, "I don't have a husband." "No, you're right," he says. "You have five husbands, and the man you're living with right now is not your husband."

What is Jesus doing? Surely here in this woman with her long and sordid sexual history we have someone who fits the traditional understanding of a "sinner." Is he trying to humiliate her? No; if that were the case, he would never have broken the social barriers of respectability and opened up the conversation with her in the gentle way he did.

Why does Jesus seem to suddenly change the subject from seeking living water to her history with men? The answer is—he isn't changing the subject. He's nudging her, saying, "If you want to understand the nature of this living water I offer, you need to first understand how you've been seeking it in your own life. You've been trying to get it through men, and it's not working, is it? Your need for men is eating you alive, and it will never stop."

At this point the woman, shocked by his knowledge of her life and his insight, responds, "Sir, I see you are a prophet!" Then she asks him one of the great theological questions of the day. "We worship at this temple here and the Jews worship at the temple in Jerusalem. Who is right?" In verses 21–24 Jesus responds with a remarkable paragraph that could be summarized like this: "The time is coming when there will be no need for a physical temple in order to have access to God." Overwhelmed, she responds, "When the Messiah comes he will explain all these things to us." Finally Jesus drops the bomb: "I, the one speaking to you—I am he" (John 4:26).

Now let us turn to the encounter Jesus had just before this one with the Outcast. In John 3, Jesus meets a very important man, a Pharisee, a religious and civic leader.

> Now there was a Pharisee, a man named Nicodemus who was a member of the Jewish ruling council. He came to Jesus at night and said, "Rabbi, we know that you are a teacher who has come from God. For no one could perform the signs you are doing if God were not with him."
>
> Jesus replied, "Very truly I tell you, no one can see the kingdom of God unless they are born again."
>
> "How can anyone be born when they are old?" Nicodemus asked. "Surely they cannot enter a second time into their mother's womb to be born!"
>
> Jesus answered, "Very truly I tell you, no one can enter the kingdom of God unless they are born of water and the Spirit. Flesh gives birth to flesh, but the Spirit gives birth to spirit. You should not be surprised at my saying, 'You must be born again.'" (John 3:1–7)

Did you notice that this is almost the opposite of how Jesus treated the woman at the well? He started off very gently with her, surprising her with his openness, and then slowly confronted her with her spiritual need. In his encounter with this Insider, however, Jesus is more forceful and direct. Nicodemus begins with courtesy: "Ah, Rabbi, I've heard many wonderful things about you. People say you have a lot of wisdom that God has given you." But Jesus confronts Nicodemus right up front, saying, "You must be born again." I suppose Nicodemus, who has spent his life worshiping God according to strict Jewish tradition, must have been offended by this strange pronouncement.

Born again. That's where this now-loaded term comes from. Who are "born-again" Christians, anyway? It's common nowadays to believe that born-again people are different from most of us—more emotional or more broken, like drug addicts or emotionally unstable people—and they need a dramatic turnaround to get them on the right path. We imagine they have done something so bad or are so weak that only a seismic change in their lives will help them. So most people today, thinking they are being tolerant, would say that maybe being born again is for people who are weaker than the rest of us and who thus need a cathartic experience. Maybe it's for people who need authority and structure in their lives, so they join regimented, authoritarian religious movements. Being born again, in other words, is for a certain kind of person. And if that's what somebody needs, then let him or her have it.

The problem with this view is that the biblical story doesn't allow us to hold it. Nicodemus is a civic leader, a member of the Sanhedrin, the assembly of Hebrew high court judges. He is prosperous. He's a devout and upstanding Pharisee; you couldn't have any more religious bona fides than that. He's not an emotional or broken type of person at all. And when Nicodemus calls Jesus—a young man with no formal training— "rabbi," this shows that he is more humble and open-minded than most of his peers. So here in Nicodemus you have an altogether admirable person—pulled together, successful, disciplined, moral, religious, yet open-minded.

And what does Jesus say? He uses a different metaphor with the Insider than the one he used with the Outcast. Rather than pressing him on his lack of satisfaction ("I can give you living water"), he's pressing him on his smug *self*-satisfaction ("You must be born again"). What did you have to do, Jesus is asking, with being born? Did you work hard to earn the privilege of being born? Did it happen due to your skillful planning? Not at all. You don't earn or contribute *anything* to being born. It is a free gift of life. And so it is with the new birth. Salvation is by grace—there are no moral efforts that can earn or merit it. You must be born again.

This is an astonishing thing to say to a man like Nicodemus. Jesus is saying that the pimps and the prostitutes outside on the street are in the same position, spiritually, as he is. There is Nicodemus, flush with his moral and spiritual accomplishments, and there is someone out on the street who is homeless and addicted, and as far as God is concerned they are equally lost. They both have to start from scratch. They both have to be born again. They both need eternal spiritual life or something will eat them alive. And that life is going to have to be a free gift.

How dare Jesus say that?

Jesus can say it because he is working on a deeper understanding of sin than most people have. Let me bring the word back now with all its cultural baggage. Look at the woman at the well. Most people probably understand why Jesus would regard her as a sinner in need of salvation. But most people can't understand why Jesus treats the Insider, Nicodemus, the way he does. Why would he be regarded as a sinner in need of salvation? Why would Jesus tell this good man that he has done essentially nothing to earn a place in heaven?

Here is the surprising answer: Sin is looking to something else besides God for your salvation. It is putting yourself in the place of God, becoming your own savior and lord, as it were. That's the biblical definition of sin, the first of the Ten Commandments. One way to do this is to break all the moral rules in your pursuit of pleasure and happiness, like the woman in the well. This makes sex or money or power into a kind of salvation. But then there is the religious way to be your own savior and lord. That is to act as if your good life and moral achievement will essentially require God to bless you and answer your prayers the way you want. In this case you are looking to your moral goodness and efforts to give you the significance and security that nonreligious people look to sex, money, and power to give them. What is insidious about this is that religious people constantly talk about trusting in God—but if you think your goodness is even contributing to your salvation, then you are actually being your own savior. You are trusting in yourself. And while you may in this case not be committing adultery or literally robbing people, your heart will increasingly be filled with such pride, self-righteousness, insecurity, envy, and spite that you make the world a miserable place to live for those around you.

So you see, Nicodemus and the Samaritan woman are equal sinners in need of grace. And so are we all. In every case, you are trying to be your own savior and lord, trying to put God in your debt, or at least trying to tilt the odds of the universe in your favor. Either way, Jesus calls it sin. He says that you need living water and that you need to be born again to get it. You need to repent, admit your need, ask God to receive you for Jesus' sake, and be converted.

Some people might say, "But I'm neither kind of person—I'm a morally good person who is not religious. There may be a God, I don't know for sure. But either way I'm a good person and that's all that should matter." Is that really all that should matter? Imagine a widow has a son she raises and puts through good schools and a good university at great sacrifice to herself, for she is a woman of very slender means. And as she's raising him she says, "Son, I want you to live a good life. I want you to always tell the truth, always work hard, and care for the poor." And after the young man graduates from college he goes off into his career and life—and never speaks to his mother or spends time with her. Oh, he may send her a card on her birthday, but he never phones or visits. What if you asked him about his relationship with his mother, and he responded: "No, I don't have anything to do with her personally. But I always tell the truth, work hard, and care for the poor. I've lived a good life—that's all that matters, isn't it?"

I doubt you would be satisfied with that answer. It is not enough for the man to merely live a moral life as his mother desired without having any kind of relationship with her. His behavior is condemnable because in fact she gave him all he has. More than just a moral life, he owes her his love and loyalty.

And if there is a God, you owe him literally everything. If there is a God, you owe him far more than a morally decent life. He deserves to be at the center of your life. Even if you are a good person but you are not letting God be God to you, you are just as guilty of sin as Nicodemus or the Samaritan woman. You are being your own savior and lord.

What is the solution? We need to stop looking to false

forms of salvation, to pseudo-saviors. If you build your life on your career, or your spouse, or your money, or your morality, and it fails, there is no hope for you. Do you know why? Because every other savior but Jesus Christ is not really a savior. If your career fails, it won't forgive you. It can only punish you with self-loathing and shame. Jesus is the only savior who if you gain him will satisfy you, and if you fail him will forgive you. Your career and your moral performance, by contrast, cannot die for your sins.

If you keep reading the fourth chapter of John, you'll see that the Samaritan woman tells her friends about the living water she has found. She testifies to meeting the Messiah and invites everyone to go meet him, too. Why did she find salvation? I'll tell you: It was because Jesus was thirsty. If he had not been thirsty, he would not have gone to the well, and she would not have found the living water. But why was Jesus thirsty? It was because the divine Son of God, the maker of heaven and earth, had emptied himself of his glory and descended into the world as a vulnerable mortal, subject to becoming weary and thirsty. In other words, she found the living water because Jesus Christ said, "I thirst." That is not the last time Jesus Christ said, "I thirst," in the book of John. On the cross just before he died, he said, "I thirst," and he meant more than just physical thirst. There Jesus was experiencing the loss of the relationship with his father because he was taking the punishment we deserved for our sins. There he was cut off from the Father, the source of living water. He was experiencing the ultimate, torturous, killing, eternal thirst of which the worst death by dehydration is just a hint. That is both paradoxical and astonishing. It is because Jesus Christ experienced cosmic thirst on the cross that you and I can have our spiritual thirst satisfied. It is because he died that we can be born again. And he did it gladly. Seeing what he did and why he did it will turn our hearts away from the things that enslave us and toward him in worship. That is the gospel, and it is the same for skeptics, believers, insiders, outcasts, and everyone in between.

THREE

※

THE GRIEVING SISTERS

Almost no one argues that the world is fine as it is and that there is nothing wrong with the human race. Just as Jesus' encounters with the woman at the well and Nicodemus show us what's wrong with the world, the story of Mary and Martha will focus on what—or who—can put it right. And the answer, Christians believe, is Jesus. So let's look at him. Who is this figure at the center of Christianity who's supposed to put everything right?

To do that, we're going to look again at the Gospel of John, which tells the story of Jesus and his relationship with two sisters, Mary and Martha, and their brother, Lazarus. Early in chapter 11, Lazarus is called someone whom Jesus loved. That is a term used in the Gospels to describe Jesus' relationship to his most intimate disciples. Apparently, Jesus, Lazarus, Mary, and Martha thought of themselves as practically family.

The Gospel account tells us that Lazarus became extremely

sick and his life hung in the balance. Mary and Martha sent for Jesus, but before he arrived, Lazarus died. When Jesus finally came to his friends' home, all were in mourning, and Lazarus's body was already in the tomb. What Jesus did next is one of the most famous incidents in history. It is also one of the most revealing, showing us not only who Jesus is but what he came to do.

On his arrival, Jesus found that Lazarus had already been in the tomb for four days. Now Bethany was less than two miles from Jerusalem, and many Jews had come to Martha and Mary to comfort them in the loss of their brother. When Martha heard that Jesus was coming, she went out to meet him, but Mary stayed at home.

"Lord," Martha said to Jesus, "if you had been here, my brother would not have died. But I know that even now God will give you whatever you ask."

And Jesus said to her, "Your brother will rise again."

Martha answered, "I know he will rise again in the resurrection at the last day."

And Jesus said to her, "I am the resurrection and the life. The one who believes in me will live, even though they die; and whoever lives by believing in me will never die. Do you believe this?"

"Yes, Lord," she replied, "I believe that you are the Messiah, the Son of God, who is to come into the world."

After she had said this, she went back and called her sister Mary aside. "The Teacher is here," she said, "and is asking for you." When Mary heard this, she got up quickly and went to him. Now Jesus had not yet entered the village, but was still at the place where Martha had met him. When the Jews who had been with Mary in the house, comforting her, noticed how quickly she got up and went out, they followed her, supposing she was going to the tomb to mourn there.

When Mary reached the place where Jesus was and saw him, she fell at his feet and said, "Lord, if you had been here, my brother would not have died."

When Jesus saw her weeping, and the Jews who had come along with her also weeping, he was deeply moved in spirit and troubled. "Where have you laid him?" he asked.

"Come and see, Lord," they replied.

Jesus wept.

Then the Jews said, "See how he loved him!" (John 11:17–36)

Martha comes to Jesus and says, "Lord, if you had been here, my brother would not have died." Just moments later,

Mary comes out and says the same thing, verbatim. Two sisters, same situation, exactly the same words. But strikingly, Jesus' responses are sharply different. When Martha speaks he almost argues with her. Her message is "You came too late," but Jesus replies, "I am the resurrection and the life! With me it's never too late." The flow of her heart is toward despair, but Jesus is pushing against that flow. He's rebuking her doubt and giving her hope. Then he sees Mary, who says exactly the same thing, but this time his response is the complete opposite. He doesn't argue; in fact he's practically speechless. And instead of pushing against the flow of her heart's sadness, he enters it. He stands alongside her in her grief. He bursts into tears and can say only, "Where is he?" Now, these radically divergent responses by Jesus are more than simply a counterintuitive curiosity. They point not only to Jesus' profound relational wisdom, but to an even deeper truth about his character and his identity.

Imagine that you were making up a story about a divine figure who had come to earth in disguise as a human being. In the story, this divine being arrives at the funeral of a friend, knowing that he has the power to raise his dead friend to life and that he is about to wipe away all the mourners' tears in the space of a few minutes. What would be this person's most likely inner emotional state? Surely you would depict him as smiling, excited, even playful. You'd expect him to be rubbing his hands with anticipation, saying under his breath, "Wait until you all see what I'm about to do!" Or perhaps you as the story writer would just keep him speaking in an elevated tone: "I am the resurrection and the life." Both of those reactions would seem to be in character for someone who claims to be divine. But we would never imagine that such a divine person would get sucked into Mary's agony and just stand there weeping. Why would he be so strong one minute and so vulnerable the next?

But this is *not* a story someone made up. And this account shows us dramatically what the New Testament says elsewhere propositionally: that Jesus is both truly God *and* fully man. Not just God, disguised as a man; not just man, with an air of deity; but the God-man. His encounters, first with Martha, then Mary, show us he is both God and human.

In his encounter with Martha he says, "I am the resurrection and the life." That's a claim of deity. Only God can give life and take it away. Notice that he's not merely saying, "I can revive Lazarus—I have special access to divine supernatural power." He's saying, "I *am* the resurrection and the life. I *am* the power that gives everything life and keeps everything alive." Astonishing.

This is by no means the only place that Jesus makes a claim like this. He points to his divinity all through the Gospels. In fact, if you include the indirect references as well as the explicit statements, these divine identity claims are in almost every chapter. In Luke 10 there's a place where Jesus makes an off-handed statement: "I saw Satan fall from heaven like lightning" (v. 18). His disciples must have been dumbfounded, thinking, "*What?!* Is he kidding? He remembers the prehistorical fall of Satan from heaven to earth? He saw that?" Another indirect claim to deity by Jesus that shocked his contemporaries was Jesus' persistent declaration of the forgiveness of sins. It is obvious to everyone that the only sin you can forgive is one committed against you. You can't forgive Jim for lying to Sam—only Sam can forgive Jim for doing that. So when Jesus tells a paralyzed man, "Son, your sins are forgiven," the onlookers rightly conclude that Jesus is claiming to be God, by implying that all sins are against *him* (Mark 2:5).

But Jesus' explicit divine claims are plentiful, too. In John 5 a crowd sought to stone him because they heard him claim to be equal with God. In John 8 they tried to do the same thing when he claimed not only to be older than Abraham but to be eternal, taking on himself the divine name. "Before Abraham was born, *I am*" (John 8:58). In John 14 he says something similar to what he says here to Martha. He claims not merely to *have* the truth but to *be* the truth—"I am the way and the truth and the life" (v. 6). In John 20, Thomas calls Jesus "my Lord and my God!" (v. 28) and Jesus accepts his worship without comment.

These claims have always posed a great challenge for readers of the Gospels, and never more so than in our current day. Most acknowledge the beauty, power, and uniqueness of Jesus' teaching. There is, therefore, a strong desire to portray Jesus as one wise religious sage among many. But nineteenth-century Scottish Presbyterian minister John Duncan (and later twentieth-century author C. S. Lewis) taught that Jesus' assertions of divine identity make that proposition impossible. The founders of every other major religion said, "I'm a prophet who shows you how to find God," but Jesus taught, "I'm God, come to find you." This means we can't look at Jesus as only one more religious teacher supplementing the world's store of wisdom. He was either a conscious fraud, was himself deluded, or was in fact divine. Duncan called this a trilemma.

Jesus then demands a radical response of some kind. You could denounce him for being evil, or you may flee from him because he's a lunatic, or you can fall down and worship him for being God. All of those reactions make sense; they are consistent with the reality of his words. But what you can't do is respond *moderately*. You must not say to him, "Nice teaching. Very helpful. You are a fine thinker." That is simply dishonest. If he's not who he says he is, then his thinking is deeply distorted and flawed. If he is who he claims to be, he is infinitely more than just a great thinker. Jesus says to us, in effect, "You have to deal with my claims. If I am wrong, I am inferior to all those other founders who had the wisdom and humility to not claim to be God. And if I'm right, I *must* be a superior way to find out who God is and what ultimate reality is. But I am certainly not equal to all others."

Now, I've talked to many people who sought to get out of

this trilemma in different ways. Maybe the most common attempt I've encountered suggests that Jesus never claimed to be God at all. "How can you trust the historical reliability of the New Testament accounts?" this objection goes. "How do you know he even existed, let alone that he made divine claims? Didn't the idea of Jesus as divine Son of God only develop many years later after his death?" Actually we have good evidence about Jesus' existence and life from historical documents outside of the Bible. Also, there is plenty of good scholarship making a convincing case that the Gospels are not oral tradition filled with legendary materials but an oral *history*, based on eyewitness accounts. And the evidence of Jesus' divine claims extends beyond the Gospel accounts themselves. Historical evidence indicates that there was never any debate or time when Christians didn't believe Jesus was God. For example, in Paul's letter to the Philippians, written only about two decades after Jesus' death, there is an early Christian hymn— probably older than the letter itself—in adoration of Christ's deity (Phil. 2:5–11). This means that belief in Jesus' divine identity did not develop long after Jesus' death, but was based on his own teaching and was the rule in the Christian community from the start.[5] So this effort to escape the trilemma does not work.

People who realize they can't escape the trilemma then go after one of the options within it: "Okay, I'll bite. Why couldn't he have been a conscious fraud? Just because he was a brilliant teacher doesn't mean he couldn't have been deceptive." But here it is important to remember that all of Jesus' first followers were Jews, and first-century Jews had a view of God that was so transcendently high that they refused to even write out or pronounce his name. Any suggestion that God could become a weak, flesh-and-blood human being would have been violently denounced. This means, first, that the idea of a God-man would never have occurred to Jewish men and women, no matter how high their regard for their leader. It means, second, that no charlatan would have even tried to convince Jewish followers he was divine. He would have known that his chances of success were nil, and history bears this out. There were other Jewish figures claiming to be the Messiah during the first century, and many of them had followings, but not a single one was ever worshipped as divine.

"Or," you may ask, "what if Jesus was not a conniver, but was truly sincere and self-deceived? What if he truly believed he was God? Isn't there a chance that he could have convinced his followers?" No, and here is why. We should reflect on the fact that no major religion has a founder who claimed to be God, though some small short-lived cults have had them. While there have been self-deceived people in history who have made divine claims, they never were able to make their assertions believable except to a tiny group. Why not? It is impossible to convince people you are God if you have any of the normal flaws of human character—selfishness, impatience, uncontrolled anger, pride, dishonesty, and cruelty. And there are invariably people who live closely enough to the divine claimant to see all of those flaws and who are thus able to see through the illusion. And if you add to this the deep cultural and theological skepticism of Judaism, you see that it would be impossible to convince a critical mass of Jews that you were God—unless that were really the most sensible explanation of the facts.

Historical scholarship shows us that, after his death, a fast-growing body of people, insisting they were faithful to Jewish monotheism, nonetheless began to worship Jesus as the one True God.[6] What kind of life must Jesus have led to accomplish what no other person in history has ever done—convince more than a tiny percentage of unbalanced people that he is the Creator and Judge of the universe? What kind of person must Jesus have been to overcome the profound resistance of Jews to such preposterous claims? The answer is, he would have to have been like the incomparably beautiful human being depicted throughout the New Testament. And we see a stunning portrait of him here.

When Jesus meets Martha we indeed get a glimpse of his deity and power—he's God. But that doesn't explain the totality of who he is. The very next moment, he breaks down sobbing beneath the weight of Mary's grief and in the shadow of the grave. You would think that if a person were really divine, he wouldn't be that emotionally exposed, but he is. So here we see deity joined to human vulnerability. His love pulls him down into weeping. Despite his claim that he *is* the resurrection and the life—that he is God—he responds to Mary in this way because he is fully human as well. He is one with us. He feels the horrific power of death and the grief of love lost.

What you have in Jesus Christ, then, is something that is pretty hard to believe, and even harder to describe. He's not 50 percent human and 50 percent God, nor is he 20 percent God and 80 percent human, or vice versa. He's not just a human being with a particularly high God consciousness or a divine figure with the illusion of a physical body. He is God but also absolutely and totally human. Now, no other religion agrees with this. No religion other than Christianity believes that the transcendent creator, the author of life, became a weak, limited mortal who felt the full horror of death. Do you believe Jesus was the God-man? I wouldn't be surprised if you struggled with that! But look at the story, watch how he actually responds to these two women, and you may see that whether you can get your mind around the idea of a divine-yet-human person, it's exactly what you most need.

Jesus gives Martha what we could call the ministry of truth. That is what she needs most at that moment. He sort of grabs her by the shoulders with truth. "Listen to me! Don't despair. I'm here. Resurrection. Life. That's what I am." Because of his divine identity, he is high enough to point her to the stars. Then, when he gets to Mary, he gives her what we could call the ministry of tears. That is what she needs most at that moment. Because of his human identity, he is low enough to step into her sorrow—with complete sincerity and integrity—and just weep with her.

Now, frankly, everybody needs a ministry of truth and a ministry of tears at different times. Sometimes you need more of the bracing truth; you need to be shaken by a loving friend who says, "Wake up and look around you." Other times you really just need somebody to weep with you. Sometimes to lay truth on people when they're grieved is absolutely wrong, but other times just to weep with them and not tell them the truth is equally wrong. None of us has the temperament or the patience or the insight to give people exactly what they need all the time. Some of us have personalities that are prone to confront even when sympathy is called for, and others of us are the opposite. But Jesus Christ is never strong when he should be tender or tender when he should be strong. Yet it isn't just that he is the perfect, wonderful counselor. He is the truth itself come in tears. He is deity incarnate in the flesh.

It is this paradox—that he is both God and human—that gives Jesus an overwhelming beauty. He is the Lion and the Lamb. Despite his high claims, he is never pompous; you never see him standing on his own dignity. Despite being absolutely approachable to the weakest and broken, he is completely fearless before the corrupt and powerful. He has tenderness without weakness. Strength without harshness. Humility without the slightest lack of confidence. Unhesitating authority with a complete lack of self-absorption. Holiness and unending convictions without any shortage of approachability. Power without insensitivity. I once heard a preacher say, "No one has yet discovered the word Jesus ought to have said. He is full of surprises, but they are all the surprises of perfection."[7]

So Jesus is God become human. But of course this leaves us with a question. Why did he do it? Why did absolute power have to enter into our weakness? Let's look at the last part of the account of the grieving sisters.

> Jesus, once more deeply moved, came to the tomb. It was a cave with a stone laid across the entrance. "Take away the stone," he said.
>
> "But, Lord," said Martha, the sister of the dead man, "by this time there is a bad odor, for he has been there four days."
>
> Then Jesus said, "Did I not tell you that if you believe, you will see the glory of God?"
>
> So they took away the stone. Then Jesus looked up and said, "Father, I thank you that you have heard me. I knew that you always hear me, but I said this for the benefit of the people standing here, that they may believe that you sent me."
>
> When he had said this, Jesus called in a loud voice, "Lazarus, come out!" The dead man came

out, his hands and feet wrapped with strips of linen, and a cloth around his face.

Jesus said to them, "Take off the grave clothes and let him go." (John 11:38–44)

I get frustrated with virtually every English translation of verse 38. Here we read it as "Jesus, once more deeply moved, came to the tomb." But this verse contains a Greek word that means "to bellow with anger," and somehow no translator feels that he or she has the freedom to say what every commentator and Greek expert says the text is saying. Jesus is absolutely furious. He's bellowing with rage—he is roaring. Who or what is he angry at? There is no indication that he's angry at the family. Then what is it?

Dylan Thomas was right: "Do not go gentle into that good night. Rage, rage against the dying of the light." Jesus is raging against *death*. He doesn't say, "Look, just get used to it. Everybody dies. That's the way of the world. Resign yourself." No, he doesn't do that. Jesus is looking squarely at our greatest nightmare—the loss of life, the loss of loved ones and of love—and he's incensed. He's mad at evil and suffering, and even though he's God, he's not mad at himself. What does that mean?

First, it means that evil and death are the result of sin and not of God's original design. He did not make a world filled with sickness, suffering, and death. But you might ask, if God is that unhappy with the world as it is, why doesn't he just show up and stop it? Why doesn't he just appear on earth and end all evil? But that question reveals a lack of self-knowledge. The Bible says—and we know deep down—that so much that is wrong with the world is wrong because of the human heart. So much of the misery of life here is due to selfishness, pride, cruelty, anger, oppression, war, and violence. Which means that if Jesus Christ had come to earth with the sword of God's wrath against evil, none of us would have been left to tell about it. We all have evil and self-centeredness deep inside us.

However, Jesus did not come with a sword in his hands; he came with nails in his hands. He did not come to bring judgment; he came to bear judgment. And this passage reveals this in the way it begins to unfold Jesus' dilemma. Later in chapter 11, when the religious leaders see what Jesus has done in this display of power, they realize this miracle made him more dangerous than they ever thought he would be. So after he raises Lazarus, the leaders have a meeting, and by verse 53, John says, "So from that day on they plotted to take his life."

Jesus knew all this, of course. He knew that if he raised Lazarus from the dead, the religious establishment would try to kill him. And so he knew the only way to bring Lazarus out of the grave was to put himself into the grave. He knew the only way to interrupt Lazarus's funeral was to summon his own. If he was going to save us from death, he was going to have to go to the cross, and bear the judgment we deserve. That's why when Jesus approached the tomb, instead of smiling at the prospect of putting on a great show, he was shaking with anger and had tears on his cheeks. He knew what it would cost him to save us from death. Maybe he was able to feel the jaws of death closing in on him. And yet knowing and experiencing all that, he cried, "Lazarus, come out."

The witnesses said about Jesus, "See how he loved Lazarus"; but really we must behold how he loves *us*. He became human, mortal, vulnerable, killable—all out of love for us.

In 1961 the Russians put a man in orbit, and afterward Russian premier Nikita Khrushchev said something bold. I remember it very well; I was eleven years old when it happened. He said something like "We have sent a man into space and we didn't see God, so we have proved there is no God." Not very solid logic or philosophy, but nonetheless, he meant it, and millions of people believe something to that effect. They think empirical observation has proven there is no God. C. S. Lewis wrote an essay about this idea called "The Seeing Eye," and in it he argued that if there were a God, we would not relate to him the way a person on the first story of a house relates to a person on the second story. The ground-floor resident can go up the steps to find the second-floor resident. But God is not someone who merely lives in the sky—he is the creator of the whole universe, earth and sky and time and space, and of us. Our relationship to God, then, is more like Shakespeare's relationship to Hamlet. How much will Hamlet know about Shakespeare? Only what Shakespeare writes about himself into the play. Hamlet will never be able to find out anything about his author any other way. In the same way, Lewis concludes, we can't find God just by going to higher altitudes. We'll only know about God if God has written something about himself into our life, into our world. And he has.

But he has not only given us information. Someone who did something like what Lewis describes was his friend, the author Dorothy Sayers. Sayers was one of the first women to go to Oxford, and she was a writer of detective fiction. She wrote a series of great stories and novels, called the Lord Peter Wimsey stories. Lord Peter was an aristocratic detective, single and alone, and in the middle of the series, a tall, not particularly attractive woman named Harriet Vane appears in the stories. Harriet is one of the first women to go to Oxford, and she is a writer of detective fiction. She and Peter fall in love, get married, and solve mysteries together. What's going on there? Some people have speculated that Dorothy Sayers looked into the world she created—and into the character she created— and saw his pain, saw his loneliness, fell in love with him, and wrote herself into the story just to save him.

God, you see, has done quite the same thing. God looked into our world—the world he made—and saw us destroying ourselves and the world by turning away from him. It filled his heart with pain (Genesis 6:6). He loved us. He saw us struggling to extricate ourselves from the traps and misery we created for ourselves. And so he wrote himself in. Jesus Christ, the God-man, born in a manger, born to die on a cross for us.

Behold who Jesus is, how he loves you and how he came to put the world right.

FOUR

THE WEDDING PARTY

We have seen in earlier chapters that Jesus came into this world because of its broken and dark condition. But in this chapter, I want to think about *how* things can be put right in the world. More pointedly, how did Jesus come to do it?

This encounter involves a wedding feast. John 2 tells us that Jesus, his mother, and some of his disciples had been invited to a particular banquet in the town of Cana. Ancient and traditional cultures put far more emphasis on the family and the community than on the individual. Meaning in life was to be found not in individual achievement but in being a good husband or wife, son or daughter, father or mother. The purpose of a marriage was not primarily the happiness of the two individuals but instead to bind the community together and to raise the next generation. In other words, the purpose of marriage was the good of the commonwealth. The bigger, the stronger, and the more numerous the families of a town, the better its economy, the greater the military security, the more everyone flourished.

And this meant that weddings and wedding feasts were a far bigger deal than they are today. Each wedding was a public feast for the entire town because marriage was about the whole community, not merely the couple. At the same time, it was also the biggest event in the personal life of both the bride and the groom. This was the day they came of age and became full adult members of their society. It is no surprise, then, that ancient wedding feasts went on for a week at least.

And with this background we can see that our text opens abruptly on a great disaster. Perhaps just a day or two into the festivities the family ran out of wine, the single most important element in an ancient feast. Essentially, the party was over. This was not a mere breach of etiquette but a social and psychological catastrophe, particularly in a traditional honor-and-shame culture.

This is the occasion for conflict between Jesus and his mother:

> On the third day a wedding took place at Cana in Galilee. Jesus' mother was there, and Jesus and his disciples had also been invited to the wedding. When the wine was gone, Jesus' mother said to him, "They have no more wine."
>
> "Woman, why do you involve me?" Jesus replied. "My hour has not yet come."

His mother said to the servants, "Do whatever he tells you."

Nearby stood six stone water jars, the kind used by the Jews for ceremonial washing, each holding from twenty to thirty gallons.

Jesus said to the servants, "Fill the jars with water"; so they filled them to the brim.

Then he told them, "Now draw some out and take it to the master of the banquet."

They did so, and the master of the banquet tasted the water that had been turned into wine. He did not realize where it had come from, though the servants who had drawn the water knew. Then he called the bridegroom aside and said, "Everyone brings out the choice wine first and then the cheaper wine after the guests have had too much to drink; but you have saved the best till now."

What Jesus did here in Cana of Galilee was the first of the signs through which he revealed his glory; and his disciples believed in him. (John 2:2–11)

Now, the key to understanding this event is the last verse. This was not called merely a miracle but a *sign*. A sign is a symbol, or signifier, of something else. Jesus did not have to exercise his power in this situation, but he did. And when he chose to do so, it became "the first of his signs through which he revealed his glory"—his true identity—to others. And the fact that he did it this way is full of interest.[8]

Consider that this is the very beginning of Jesus' career, of his public ministry. Imagine you are a candidate for office, an entrepreneur launching a brand, or a musician releasing your first major recording. In every case, you will choose your first public presentation with enormous care. Each detail will be carefully controlled so that every single thing you say and do will convey the message of what you are about. But look at this calling card, as it were, of Jesus'. Nobody's dying, nobody's possessed by demons, nobody's starving. Why would Jesus decide that a quintessential signifier of all he is about would be to keep a party going? Why would his first miracle—a signifying miracle, according to John—use supernatural power to bring a lot of great wine to sustain the festivities? Why in the world would he do that?

Reynolds Price, who was a very prominent professor of English literature at Duke University for many years and a celebrated novelist, wrote an interesting book called *Three Gospels* in which he translated and analyzed the Gospels of Mark and John and then wrote his own version of the life of Jesus. Speaking as a literature expert, he argues that the Gospel of John was not a work of fiction but rather was written by "the hand of a clear-minded thoughtful eyewitness to the acts and mind of Jesus."[9] One of the many reasons for his conclusion is this account of the first miracle. Price asks: "Why invent—for the inaugural sign of Jesus' great career—a miraculous solution to a mere social oversight?"[10] No one would have made something like that up!

Now, as we have already seen, Price is exaggerating a bit. To people in this culture, running out of wine was more than a mere social embarrassment. Still, for all the shame the bride and groom must have felt, it was not a life-and-death situation, so you feel the force of Price's question. What did this act signify about what Jesus came into this world to do?

First, let's look at what Jesus brought to this situation (and to us). In verse 9 we are introduced to the "master of the banquet." He was essentially a master of ceremonies, a presider. It was his job to call people to celebrate and to make sure the conditions for that celebration were all in place. Bottom line: It was his job to make the party great. And when Jesus turns water into wine and saves the day, do you see what Jesus is saying? He is saying, as it were, *I* am the true master of the banquet. I am Lord of the Feast.

"Wait," someone says. "I thought he came to humble himself, to lose his glory, then to be rejected and to go to the cross." Of course that is right, but in a way, Jesus is putting even that terrible loss and pain into context.

"Yes," he is saying, "I'm going to suffer. Yes, there's going to be self-denial. Yes, there's going to be sacrifice—for me first and then for my followers as well. But it's all a means to an end, which is festival joy! It's all in order to bring about resurrection and the new heavens and new earth. The end of all evil and death and tears. You know all those Dionysian legends about the forest running with wine, dancing, and music? That's nothing compared to the eternal feast that is coming at the end of history. And those who believe in me will have within them a stream of that joy, a foretaste of that joy, now. A taste that will be profoundly consoling and refreshing in the hardest and driest of times—like living water. That, ultimately, is what I've come to bring. That's why this is my first sign."

Indeed, the Bible often uses sensory language to talk about God's salvation and even God himself. In Psalm 34 the author David says to his Israelite readers, "Taste and see that the Lord is good" (v. 8). But don't they already know that the Lord is good? Yes, they do, but when David invites them to "taste" he wants them to go beyond mental assent to a proposition, however true it may be. "Of course you *know* that the Lord is good," David is saying, "but I want you to *taste* it." He wants them to experience it deeply.

I am a Presbyterian minister; and for me to say, "Jesus Christ comes to bring transporting joy and deep heart fulfillment, not only later but now," can seem a little odd to some people. Presbyterians have a reputation of being a little more buttoned-up than that. But the Bible gives me no choice. Do you know what the Bible says about the last day, at the end of time? Jesus may have been thinking about that at this moment in the wedding. Isaiah 25:6–8 says, "On this mountain the

Lord Almighty will prepare a feast of rich food for all peoples, a banquet of aged wine—the best of meats and the finest of wines. On this mountain he will destroy the shroud that enfolds all peoples, the sheet that covers all nations; he will swallow up death forever. The Sovereign Lord will wipe away the tears from all faces; he will remove his people's disgrace from all the earth. The Lord has spoken."

In J. R. R. Tolkien's *Lord of the Rings*, when Samwise Gamgee wakes up having been rescued from the fires of Mount Doom and he sees Gandalf still alive, he realizes what has happened. He says, "Gandalf, I thought you were dead. But then I thought I was dead. Is everything sad going to come untrue?" The whole Bible says that's essentially what Jesus is going to do in the end. We're not going to be taken out of this world into heaven, but heaven is going to come down at the end of time to renew this world. Every tear will be wiped away. In essence, everything sad is going to come untrue. That's what he came to do.

In Fyodor Dostoyevsky's great novel *The Brothers Karamazov*, there is a scene in which two people are talking about suffering. Ivan Karamazov is talking about there being any possibility that we can make sense of suffering, and here's what he says:

> "I believe like a child that suffering will be healed
> and made up for, that all the humiliating absurdity

of human contradictions will vanish like a pitiful mirage, like the despicable fabrication of the impotent and infinitely small Euclidean mind of man, that in the world's finale, at the moment of eternal harmony, something so precious will come to pass that it will suffice for all hearts, for the comforting of all resentments, for the atonement of all the crimes of humanity, of all the blood that they've shed; that it will make it not only possible to forgive but to justify all that has happened."[11]

That's Dostoyevsky's Christianity surging through his literary imagination and craft. He says that he believes that at the end the reality will be so astonishing, the joy will be so incredible, the fulfillment will be so amazing that the most miserable life will feel (as St. Teresa of Ávila was reputed to have said) "like one night in a bad hotel."

Jesus Christ says, "I am the Lord of the Feast. In the end, I come to bring joy. That's the reason my calling card, my first miracle, is to set everyone laughing."

That tells us what he came to bring; but why did he have to bring it? Let's notice another detail of this miracle. He's going to rescue this young bride and groom from their gaffe, but how will he do it? By filling up jars used by the Jews for ceremonial washing. You know that Old Testament Judaism contained a great number of rites and regulations, which required many and various courses of physical cleansing and purification, all in order to point to our spiritual need. These vividly got across the idea that God is holy and perfect and we are flawed and that to connect with him at all, there needs to be atonement, cleansing, and pardon. We cannot just walk right into his presence. So Jews had many purification rites leading up to the blood sacrifices. That's what the jars were normally used for.

And here we should remember that the failure of the wine supply was more than a mere embarrassment. Imagine how deep the humiliation can be if you've let your family down in a shame-and-honor culture. We don't understand that dynamic very well today in the individualistic West. But these young people were facing certain public shame and guilt. Jesus Christ rescues them from all of that. And by employing the jars normally used for ceremonial washing, he is saying that he has come into the world to accomplish *in reality* what the ceremonial and sacrificial laws of the Old Testament pointed to. How is that so?

In chapter 2, I talk about the idea of sin. I know the term grates on us, and it's natural to squirm when a minister talks about it, but we can't understand the joy Jesus is going to bring unless we understand sin. We must understand that we are stained, that we need to be purified, that we have guilt and shame, and we need to be rescued from it—not conned into believing it doesn't exist. Allow me to be direct and personal.

You actually do know deep down that something is really wrong with you. Why are you working so hard? Why do you need to be right all the time? Why do you worry so much about how you look? It's because you know there is something wrong and you're trying to purify yourself, prove yourself, cover it up.

Do you remember the first Rocky film? Just before Rocky's big fight with the heavyweight champion, Apollo Creed, he is lying beside his girlfriend, Adrian, and says that he doesn't actually need to win the fight, just stay on his feet to the end, just go the distance. He explains:

> "I just wanna prove somethin'—I ain't no bum. . . .
> It don't matter if I lose. . . . Don't matter if he opens
> my head. . . . The only thing I wanna do is go the
> distance—that's all. Nobody's ever gone fifteen
> rounds with Creed. If I go them fifteen rounds, an'
> that bell rings an' I'm still standin', I'm gonna know
> then I weren't just another bum from the neighbor-
> hood."

I propose to you: One of the reasons you have all these dreams of working hard to look good and do well and achieve is because you are trying to prove to yourself and everyone else, even people who may not be around anymore, that you are not a bum.

Or remember Harold Abrahams from the movie *Chariots of Fire*. What was driving him to be the best at the hundred-meters sprint? Just before the final race he says, "I'll raise my eyes and look down that corridor . . . with ten lonely seconds to justify my whole existence." He's simply being candid about something that a lot of us do not want to be candid about. We do not want only to do well. We do not want just to make a contribution to society. We do not want just to make our mark. Deep down inside, we feel—no, we even know—that somehow we are bums. Another way to put it, if you want biblical imagery, is to go back to Genesis 3 when Adam and Eve eat the apple, turn away from God, and immediately feel naked. They feel they have to cover up, that they can't let even God see what they are like. So they put fig leaves on themselves. Consider the possibility that your success in life is just a big fig leaf. Consider the fact that in the end it will never be enough to cover up what you know is wrong with you.

I firmly believe we know we need to be cleansed, even those of us who are very uneasy with the idea of sin. It's awkward to put it so boldly, but there is more self-centeredness, more sin, in us than we want to believe. There's plenty in you that you would like to deny, theologically and philosophically. Ah, you will say, "I am a humanist, I don't believe that human beings are inherently evil." But if you live long enough and you are honest enough with yourself, you will learn beyond any doubt that there are things in your heart that will bite you and even shock you. You'll say, "I didn't know I was capable of that."

The problem, actually, is that we are all capable of that. Adolf Eichmann was one of the Nazi architects of the Holocaust who escaped after World War II to South America, where he was caught in 1960 and taken back to Israel for a trial. He was tried, found guilty, and executed. But there was a very interesting incident during the trial. They had to find witnesses who saw him commit the terrible crimes against humanity he was charged with. They needed to find people who saw him participate in atrocities at the death camps. One of the material witnesses was a man named Yehiel De-Nur, and when he came in to testify, he saw Eichmann in the glass booth and immediately broke down, falling to the ground and sobbing. There was pandemonium. The judge was hammering to get order. It was very dramatic.

Sometime later De-Nur was interviewed by Mike Wallace on *60 Minutes*. Wallace showed De-Nur the tape of him falling down and asked him why it happened. Was he overwhelmed by painful memories? Or with hatred? Is that why he collapsed? De-Nur said no—and then said something that probably shocked Wallace and should shock almost all secular Western people. He said that he was overcome by the realization that Eichmann was not some demon but was an ordinary human being. "I was afraid about myself. . . . I saw that am capable to do this . . . exactly like he."[12]

You can choose to say the Nazis were subhuman, that they were nothing like us, and that we are not capable of doing what they did. But there are serious problems with that view. The scariest thing about that whole chapter of history is not the few individual evil architects of it but the complicity of vast numbers of people across a society that was producing so much of the world's best scholarship, science, and culture. That makes it impossible to write off the whole era as the work of a couple of isolated monsters. Besides that, to call the Nazis "subhuman" or "not like us" is in fact the very reasoning that led the Nazis into their unthinkable atrocities. They, too, thought that certain classes of people were subhuman and beneath them. Are you prepared to deny our common humanity with them? Do you want to make the same move that they did? The vast majority of the Nazis and the millions of people who were led by them were not monsters with fangs. Hannah Arendt, watching Eichmann during the trial, reported to *The New Yorker* that he was by no means psychopathic, that he exhibited no hatred or anger. Instead he was an ordinary man who had wanted to build a career. She called this "the banality of evil." Evil lurks in the heart of all quite ordinary human beings.

So it would actually be more honest to say, "I'm somehow the same as those who have done terrible things. I am made of the same human stuff. There must be something down deep in me that is capable of great cruelty and selfishness, and I don't want to see it." Jesus of course knows that it is in there. "Many . . . believed in his name. But Jesus did not entrust himself to them . . . for he knew what was in each person" (John 2:23–25). And while, for most of us, the self-centeredness and sin of our hearts has not led to overtly criminal acts of violence and cruelty, it has still caused misery for the people around us, and it has kept us from serving the God who created us and to whom we owe everything. And Jesus came to cleanse us of this, to purify us from what is spiritually wrong with us.

So, finally, how does Jesus bring that healing, that cleansing, that forgiveness? Here we get to the narrative heart of the passage. Mary tells Jesus that the party is out of wine. It is possible that she is just telling him along with others, but unlikely. Mary may not know exactly who Jesus is, but she knows that her son is no ordinary man. She remembers the angels, of course. How could she not? And we don't know much about what else she had heard or seen in him since his birth.[13]

So she tells him about the problem. And he replies, "Woman, why do you involve me?" That appears to be a pretty cold way to talk to your mother. Sometimes with a passage like this, the translation just comes out wrong in English, and you can get a more nuanced reading from the original languages. But in this case the commentators will tell you that this is indeed an unusually insensitive way for Jesus to be addressing his mother, especially in that sort of family-oriented society.

What's happening? We know from the rest of the Gospel accounts that Jesus is not easily irritated. He doesn't say things he regrets. Even when he is being tortured he never speaks a harsh or angry word, so this is not just a bad mood. Something is weighing heavily on him. And then he lets us know what it is. He says, "My hour has not yet come."

Now, if you read the book of John carefully, you'll discover that Jesus refers to his "hour" several other times, and every time he is speaking about the occasion of his death. His hour is the moment of his death on the cross. Knowing that, do you see why this exchange is such a *non sequitur*?

Mary says, "What a disaster. They've run out of wine." To which Jesus says, "Why are you telling me this? I'm not ready to die." What?

It is very unlikely that Mary knew what "the hour" meant, and so all she knows is that her son's response to a simple statement is emotional, sharp, enigmatic, and somewhat offensive. But she doesn't argue, or ask him to explain, or walk away in disgust like most parents would. She remembers what the angels told her and so she goes to the domestic servants attending to the guests at the feast and says, "Whatever he tells you to do, do it."

But what is Jesus thinking? Why does he connect a simple request for wine with the hour of his death? Well, think of the symbolism. The miracle will be a sign of what he has come to do. What does the wine represent in his mind? What is missing from the picture that's necessary to turn the shame to joy? We know because he creates the wine in the jars for purification and cleansing.

You see, when Jesus makes his enigmatic statement it's as if he were looking far away, past his mother and past the bride and groom and past the whole wedding scene. He's seeing something else. He's thinking, "Yes, I can bring festival joy to this world; I can cleanse humankind from its guilt and shame. I have come into the world to bring joy, but, oh, Mother. I'm going to have to die to do it."

I actually think that there may be even more going on in his mind than this. In the Old Testament, God wants to show us that he doesn't want to relate to us only as a king relates to his subjects but as a groom relates to his bride. He wants a love relationship with us, as profound as the relationship between a husband and a wife. So often in the Hebrew Scriptures God presents himself as the bridegroom of his people. Then at one point in John's Gospel, in the New Testament, the disciples are criticized for not fasting, and Jesus says, "Why should the friends of the bridegroom fast when the bridegroom is still with them?" Did you hear that? Jesus calls himself the bridegroom! He does so in full awareness that, according to the Scriptures, only the creator, God of the universe, is the husband of his people. As a writer, John goes on to make much of this theme; in his book of Revelation at the end of the New Testament, he depicts the end of all things this way: "I saw the Holy City, the new Jerusalem, come down out of heaven from God, prepared as a bride beautifully dressed for her husband" (Revelation 21:2). "Then the angel said to me, 'Write this: Blessed are those who are invited to the wedding supper of the Lamb!'" (Revelation 19:9). In other words, at the end of time, there will be the feast to end all feasts. It will not be simply a generic banquet, but a wedding feast. It celebrates at long last the intimate and permanent union of people who love each other. And this is how history ends; this is what Jesus came to accomplish. We, the bride, the people Jesus has loved, will finally be united with him. The most rapturous love of a wedded couple on earth is just the dimmest hint and echo of that cosmic future reality.

Jesus is absolutely saturated in the Old Testament Scriptures, and he identifies as the Great Bridegroom, though all his work is still ahead of him. So now he finds himself at a wedding feast. What do single people think about at weddings? Why do they often sit at wedding receptions with this funny, faraway look in their eyes? They are looking beyond the current bride and groom and thinking about what their own wedding day will be like! And perhaps this is what Jesus is doing. Maybe he is thinking of his own wedding, with infinite joy and utter horror at the same time. And so let's paraphrase what he is saying one more time: "Mother, for *my* people to fall into *my* arms, I'm going to have to die. For my people to drink the cup of joy and festival blessing, I'm going to have to drink the cup of justice and punishment and death."

So here is the answer to the final question. How is Jesus going to bring us our joy? By losing all of his. By leaving his heavenly existence with his Father. By leading a lonely, misunderstood life. By going to the cross and dying in our place.

Many people say, "I don't like the church and I don't accept Christian doctrine. I don't believe in hell and God's wrath and blood atonement and all of that. But I really like Jesus. Look at how he loves people, how he gives to people. If people just imitated Jesus and followed his teaching, the world would be a better place." The problems with that view, as common as it is, are many and profound. If Jesus was thinking about his death at a wedding feast, that meant he was nearly always thinking about his death. He did *not* come primarily to be a good example. And I'm glad he didn't. Do you know why? He's too good! He's so perfect that as an example he just crushes you into the ground. Anyone who really, seriously, seeks to make him a life model, who pays attention to the details of his character and practice, will despair. He is infinitely beyond us, and comparing yourself to him will only grind your genuine aspirations to moral excellence into hopelessness.

But we see here that he did not come to tell us how to save ourselves but to save us himself. He came to die, to shed his blood, to take the cup of curse and punishment so we can raise the cup of blessing and love.

This centrality of Jesus' death is a most important insight

for understanding the Gospels. Another is the meaning and purpose of Jesus' death, namely substitution. By choosing the ceremonial jars, Jesus was signaling something that the book of Hebrews expounds at great length: that Jesus fulfilled the whole Old Testament sacrificial system. The tabernacle and the temple, the veil, the inner chamber called the Holy of Holies—at the heart of that system was a blood sacrifice. Why? Because I'm a sinner and sin needs to be punished. Something atones for my sin. Something dies in my place. The question over all those centuries when animals were being slaughtered could have been, how can a lamb take a man's place? Yet when John the Baptist sees Jesus for the first time, he says, "Behold the Lamb of God who takes away the sin of the world." In other words, John realized, all those little lambs could not and did not take away our sins. But they were pointing to the truly innocent, unblemished One, Jesus, who does. Jesus Christ came to die in our place and to take our punishment.

Many people respond to this by saying, "That's awful. Here you are, bringing us back to the bloodthirsty gods of old." Look at the *Iliad*; there's Agamemnon trying to get to Troy. He can't get there. So he sacrifices his daughter to the gods. And the gods say, "Oh, okay. That assuages our wrath against you, Agamemnon. Now we'll give you fair winds." Is that the kind of thing the Bible is talking about?

When we contemporary people hear about Jesus Christ coming here and dying, and his followers invoking the wrath of God, it seems on the surface to be just another primitive religion with slaughter and sacrifice at its center. But that completely misunderstands the gospel. If Jesus Christ is who he says he is—the creator of the universe, come in flesh—then what we really have on the cross is God himself coming to earth and paying the ultimate price with his own life. He doesn't make us pay; he pays the debt. Some have called this "the self-substitution of God."

Do you find that illogical? Think about it in terms of your own experience of forgiveness. If someone knocks over your lamp and breaks it, she says, "I'm sorry. Let me repay you. Let me replace it." Now you have a choice in how to respond. You can say, "Yes, thank you." You can make her pay. Or you can say, "No, don't mention it," and forgive her. But even if you forgive her, you're not finished. Either you have to replace the lamp or you have to go without a lamp. In other words, either that person pays or you pay. The debt doesn't vanish. Somebody always pays. If you have a lot of money, it might be easy to say, "Don't worry about it; it's nothing." But if you don't have a lot of money, and that lamp was an heirloom passed down for generations in your family, it might be harder to give that response.

The thought experiment can get trickier. If someone hurts your reputation—really wrongs you—what are you going to do? One way you can respond is to go to other people to whom that person has slandered you and ruin that person's reputation in return. An eye for an eye, and a tooth for a tooth. In other words, you could make him pay. Or you could forgive him. And if you do so, you absorb that debt. You lose face with certain people. You give up the right to ruin his reputation. In short, you suffer. You cannot truly forgive a debt without taking it on yourself.

In all this we reflect a little of the nature of God. As a holy and just God, he can't just look down at us and say, "Look at you ruining each other's lives, destroying my creation, destroying each other. I'll just let it pass." God cannot just wish away the debt, and it's not because he doesn't love you enough. Actually, it's quite the opposite. God is so holy he had to come in the form of Jesus Christ and die to pay the debt, but he is so loving he was glad to come and die for you.

Now let me appeal to you. Is there anything offensive about the idea of substitutionary sacrifice? Is there anything wrong about it in its essence? I don't think so. There's no more moving narrative than someone willingly giving up something vitally important for the betterment of someone else. There is no more heart-melting joy than to know that someone has sacrificed for you. In *A Tale of Two Cities*, Sydney Carton and Charles Darnay love the same woman, but she marries Charles. By the end of the book, Charles is arrested and put in a dungeon. He is set to be executed the next day. He has a wife and child and is going to die within twenty-four hours. Sydney, who looks just enough like Charles, sneaks into the prison and knocks out his former rival, has his friends take him to safety, puts on the other man's clothes, and stays there to die in his place.

Later, we are introduced to a waifish seamstress, also a prisoner, who is on her way to the guillotine. She walks up to the man she thinks is Charles and asks him to comfort her, until she realizes it is not Charles. Her eyes get really big and she whispers, "Are you dying for him?" And hushing her, he says, "And for his wife and child." Then, having asked him earlier to comfort her, she begs again, "O will you let me hold your brave hand, stranger?" She is warmed against the chill and steeled against death by the mere idea of his substitutionary sacrifice, and it wasn't even for her. How would you be transformed if you came to believe that Jesus Christ did it for you personally? That's what Jesus came to bring for everyone. And that's how he came to bring it. Through substitutionary sacrifice, not just to free you from guilt, but eventually to fall into his arms at the end of time, to be his spouse, so that he could love you and perfect you.

Let me offer a couple of practical thoughts. First, every time God chooses a metaphor to help us see him better, it also shows us how he sees us. If he is like our bridegroom, then if you give yourself to Jesus in faith, it means he must really delight in us. Every time God chooses an image for himself, he is saying something about us. Do you know what the bride looks like to the bridegroom as she walks down the aisle? She wears the most beautiful garments and jewels, and when he lays his eyes on her, he is absolutely delighted in her. And he wants to give her the world. How dare Jesus Christ use a metaphor like this, evoking this powerful human experience? Could it be that he loves his own like that? That he delights in you like that? Yes, he does. How different would your life be if you lived in moment-by-moment existential awareness of that?

Second, deal with the present by looking to the future. Years ago I heard Edmund Clowney preach a sermon on this text. He was reflecting on the fact that in the midst of all the joy of that wedding feast, when others were drinking wine, Jesus was in a sense tasting the bitterness of the death that lay before him. But we don't have to do that. Dr. Clowney put it something like this: "Jesus sat amidst all the joy of the wedding feast sipping the coming sorrow so that today you and I who believe in him can sit amidst all this world's sorrow sipping the coming joy." We can have enormous stability because of the coming joy, the Lamb's party. Every time you participate in the Lord's Supper by faith, you are getting a foretaste of that incredible feast. Even if right now you are in the midst of sorrow, sip the coming joy. There is only one love, only one feast, only one thing that can really give your heart all that it needs, and they all await you. Knowing that, you possess something that will enable you to face anything.

FIVE

❋

THE FIRST CHRISTIAN

In the last chapter we looked at how Jesus makes right what has gone wrong with the world. Now we're going to look at how we should respond to what he's done, which brings us to the most foundational aspect of a relationship with Christ— faith. Every place we turn in the Bible we are told that all the insights, comforts, and gifts that God can give us through Christ will come to us through faith. But there is a great deal of confusion about what Christian faith even means. To get a better understanding of this crucial concept, let's take a look at another encounter between Jesus Christ and an individual in the Gospel of John:

> Early on the first day of the week, while it was still dark, Mary Magdalene went to the tomb and saw that the stone had been removed from the entrance.
> So she came running to Simon Peter and the

other disciple, the one Jesus loved, and said, "They have taken the Lord out of the tomb, and we don't know where they have put him!"

So Peter and the other disciple started for the tomb.

Both were running, but the other disciple outran Peter and reached the tomb first.

He bent over and looked in at the strips of linen lying there but did not go in.

Then Simon Peter came along behind him and went straight into the tomb. He saw the strips of linen lying there, as well as the cloth that had been wrapped around Jesus' head. The cloth was still lying in its place, separate from the linen.

Finally the other disciple, who had reached the tomb first, also went inside. He saw and believed.

[They still did not understand from Scripture that Jesus had to rise from the dead.] Then the disciples went back to where they were staying.

Now Mary stood outside the tomb crying. As she wept, she bent over to look into the tomb and saw two angels in white, seated where Jesus' body had been, one at the head and the other at the foot.

They asked her, "Woman, why are you crying?"

"They have taken my Lord away," she said, "and I don't know where they have put him."

At this, she turned around and saw Jesus standing there, but she did not realize that it was Jesus.

He asked her, "Woman, why are you crying? Who is it you are looking for?"

Thinking he was the gardener, she said, "Sir, if you have carried him away, tell me where you have put him, and I will get him."

Jesus said to her, "Mary."

She turned toward him and cried out in Aramaic, "Rabboni!" [which means "Teacher"].

Jesus said, "Do not hold on to me, for I have not yet ascended to the Father. Go instead to my brothers and tell them, 'I am ascending to my Father and your Father, to my God and your God.'"

Mary Magdalene went to the disciples with the news: "I have seen the Lord!" And she told them that he had said these things to her. (John 20:1–18)

From the first part of this passage we learn that Christian faith is both impossible and rational. What do I mean by that? I don't mean that it is impossible for anyone to have Christian faith. What I am saying is that, in our current state of flawed moral and spiritual sensibility, no one has within them the ability to produce vibrant faith in Christ. Faith is, therefore, impossible for anyone without outside intervention or help.

Here's how the passage conveys this truth. We must keep in mind that Jesus had been telling his disciples over and over that he would die and then rise on the third day. This is particularly striking in the Gospel of Mark. In chapter 8 of Mark's Gospel he says, "The Son of Man . . . must be killed and after three days rise again." Then in chapter 9 of Mark he says, "The Son of Man . . . They will kill him, and after three days he will rise." Again in chapter 10 he says, "The Son of Man . . . they will . . . kill him. Three days later he will rise." Jesus' claim was so widely known that his enemies heard of it and stationed a guard at the tomb (Matthew 27:62–66).

And yet despite these warnings, when Mary Magdalene comes to Jesus' tomb, she sees the stone rolled away. She immediately runs back and says, "They've taken the body." Mary would have heard Jesus' prediction of his resurrection as often as anyone else. Why, when she sees the empty tomb, doesn't she even say to herself, "Oh! He said he would rise! Could it possibly be?" No. That doesn't even occur to her.

I'm going to come back later to the specific reasons why all of these first-century Jews would have been convinced that a resurrection was impossible and that Jesus couldn't have risen from the dead. But for now I'd like to pull back and make the larger point this narrative shows us—that belief in the person and work of Christ does not come naturally to anyone. Some theologians call this "inability." You may know that different theological traditions in Christianity have somewhat varied views on the degree to which we have the ability to respond to God. But all of them agree that we can't produce saving faith in Jesus Christ *solely* through our own ability. All the compelling evidence for Christianity may be laid out in front of us. The message might be as clear as can be. But there is in every human being an inherent spiritual blindness. We can't see the truth. We can't connect it to ourselves. As Exhibit A, here we witness the aftermath of the greatest act of redemption in history—God breaking the power of sin and death through the resurrection of Jesus Christ. And this had been accompanied by months and years of teaching by Jesus about this event and its meaning. And yet here is Mary staring right at it—the empty tomb—and yet she can't "see" it. She can't process it at all. And so faith is impossible without supernatural intervention by God himself.

Thomas Nagel, a prominent American philosopher, wrote a book some years ago called *The Last Word*, which deals with epistemology, the study of how we know what we know. Nagel, who calls himself a secular atheist, says that belief in God makes people nervous because of the "fear of religion." "In speaking of the fear of religion," he writes, "I don't mean to refer to the entirely reasonable hostility toward certain established religion and religious institutions, in virtue of their objectionable moral doctrine, social policies, and political influence." In other words, he argues, people have every right to hate the church for what it believes and how it behaves. But then he says, "I am talking instead of something much deeper [in us]—namely, the fear of religion itself. I speak from experience, being strongly subject to this fear myself." Finally he concludes:

> I want atheism to be true, and I am made uneasy by the fact that some of the most intelligent and well-informed people I know are religious believers. It isn't just that I don't believe in God and, naturally, hope that I'm right in my belief. It's that I hope there is no God! I don't want there to be a God; I don't want the universe to be like that. My guess is that this cosmic authority problem is not a rare condition. . . . I am curious, . . . whether there is anyone who is genuinely indifferent as to whether there is a God.

Everybody knows that there are emotional and psychological reasons why you might want to believe in God. In fact many skeptics at some point make the argument that believing in God is simply an intense form of wish fulfillment. But seldom do people point out that we all have enormous emotional and psychological reasons to *dis*believe in God. How so? In looking at a book like the Bible or at a message like the gospel, anyone sees fairly quickly that if it were true you would lose some control over how you can live your life. Who can say they're objective and neutral about *that* proposition? Thomas Nagel is honestly acknowledging this. He knows he can't say, "I am completely objective and indifferent in looking for the evidence for God, but I just don't have enough evidence." I hope you see that no one can truly say such a thing with integrity. We all have deep layers of prejudice working against the idea of a holy God who can make ultimate demands on us. And if you won't acknowledge that, you're never going to get close to objectivity. Never.

Let's say you're a judge and suddenly a case comes before you concerning a company in which you own stock. And the decision will have a huge impact on the price of the stock. Would you be allowed, or would you allow yourself, to rule in the case? No, because you couldn't possibly be objective when you know that if the decision goes a certain way, you're going to lose all of your money. So the law requires that you recuse yourself. Here's the problem: With Christianity, we're all in that very position. When it comes time to decide whether its claims are right or wrong, you have at least some vested interest in them being wrong. But you don't get to recuse yourself; you can only look at the evidence. Therefore, I'd like to suggest some ways to deal with this dilemma.

First of all, doubt your doubts. Be skeptical of your own skepticism. Why? Because you must realize that you are not completely objective. Maybe you have a very religious parent whom you dislike. Or you may have had a bad experience with an inconsistent and insensitive group of Christians. On top of that, as we have observed, few people can entertain an invitation to give up their freedom without some prejudice against it. You're afraid of the claims of Christianity being true—that's fine. If we're honest, we all are. You'll never be fair-minded with the evidence if you don't acknowledge that you can't be perfectly fair-minded. So what should you do about this? To begin, you could simply slow down, so you don't come so quickly to skeptical conclusions. Also, you should recognize that if Christianity is true, it is not just a set of rational, philosophical principles to adopt—it is a personal relationship to enter. So, to take seriously at least the possibility that it is true, why not consider praying? Why not say, "God, I don't know if you're there but I do know what prejudice is like, and I'm willing to be suspicious of it. Therefore, if you are there and if I am prejudiced, help me get through it." Break the ice with Jesus—talk to him. No one has to know you are doing it. If you're not willing to do that, I suggest that you're not willing to own the prejudice that we all start with.

But a lot of people have the opposite problem: They are actually overly anxious about having enough faith. They are too concerned about their doubts. Often I've had people say to me, "I'm interested and motivated to be a Christian, but I'm afraid my motives aren't right," or "I'm not sure I have enough faith to be a Christian." They think faith depends on getting their mind and heart in the right state. In the end, just like the first group, they are making the mistake of relying too much on themselves. They don't see what this passage teaches—you aren't capable of belief without outside help, without intervention by God, without Jesus coming to you and helping you, as he helps Mary in all of her consternation. See, Mary didn't believe until Jesus met her. She was agitated, panicking, in tears, and not able to see Jesus right before her eyes. But Jesus clears her mind and assures her heart. You will need his personal help, too, so ask him for it. In fact, if you are very concerned about finding faith in Jesus, that might be a sign that he is already helping you get there. We aren't even capable of truly wanting Jesus without his help. A sense of Jesus' absence might be a sign of his presence—a sign that he's working already in your life. As in Mary's case, Jesus might be at your side right now and you can't see it.

So, in ourselves, faith is impossible. And yet, as Jesus says, "With man this is impossible, but with God all things are possible" (Matthew 19:26).

The other thing we see in this passage is that faith is rational. It is critical to recognize this, because we have just spent time showing that faith is not *merely* a rational process—it is a supernatural and personal encounter with Jesus himself. But while Christian faith is much more than being rational, it is certainly not less than rational. By this I mean that faith is based on evidence, and right before us we have some of the most important evidence the Bible offers us.

Why aren't Mary, John, and Peter camped out at the tomb around the clock? If you don't know much about first-century culture and history, you might be surprised that Jesus would have said over and over again, "I'm going to rise on the third day," and then, despite all that repetition, we see that on the third day the disciples are not waiting around the tomb eagerly. Even Mary Magdalene, though passionately devoted to her teacher, runs away without considering the possibility that there has been a resurrection when she sees the empty tomb. Why weren't they waiting to see a miracle? Hadn't they seen him do enough miracles that they could expect him to come up with one more big one?

If you read N. T. Wright's *The Resurrection of the Son of God*, the best book written on the resurrection in at least a hundred years, you'll realize that neither Jews nor Greeks nor Romans thought the bodily resurrection of an individual was possible. The Greeks (and later the Romans) believed that all things physical, including the body, were the source of weakness and evil, and the spirit the source of strength and goodness. And so salvation was the liberation of the soul from the body. The resurrection of the body in that view would not be a desirable thing at all. What god would want to do such a thing?

The Jews, on the other hand, didn't all share that particular view of the body. They saw the material world as part of God's good creation, and some Jews (though not all) believed that at the end of time there would be a general resurrection of the righteous. But nobody—Jew, Greek, or Roman—believed God would raise an individual from the dead right in the midst of history. What's more, Jews were the last people on earth to believe that a human being could be the Son of God who should be worshipped. They'd been taught all of their lives that a human being could not be God. They had an utterly transcendent view of God. Put all these factors together and you'll see why, for first-century Jews, the idea of Jesus' resurrection simply wasn't conceivable. Despite all his predictions, it was just too incredible for them to believe or even to wish for.

We modern readers think of ancient people as being very superstitious, and that is right to a great degree. Ancient people believed all sorts of claims about magic, miracles, supernatural beings, and powers that we don't believe today. And, we reason, therefore Jesus' followers would have been very gullible about the claim of his resurrection. They would have eagerly expected it and then, if anyone at all gave out even the most fragmentary claim of having seen Jesus, thousands of credulous people would have instantly accepted it as a truth to be proclaimed.

The problem with this theory is that it is all wrong. The Gospel accounts of the resurrection do not show the disciples expecting the resurrection at all. Ironically, the disciples were just as incredulous as modern people would be. They required the same kind of multiple sightings and hands-on, eyewitness experience that we would require in order to convince them that Jesus was really alive. And in this respect the narratives fit perfectly with what we know historically of those cultures. N. T. Wright tells us at great length that, while these ancient cultures did not hold, as modern people do, that miracles in general cannot happen, resurrection was equally implausible and unimaginable to them as it is for most people today.

My question to you, then, goes like this: If you are a typical modern person, you have a worldview that insists that a bodily resurrection of a truly dead man, with his fatal wounds still visible, is simply impossible. Now imagine what kind of evidence *you* would need to knock down your doubts, to shatter your presumptions regarding this event. What kind of evidence would you need in order to believe that Jesus Christ was the Son of God, resurrected from the dead? Whatever that evidence is, you can reasonably conclude that they must have had something like it. And if that's so, the evidence that convinced them and brought them to faith might be enough to convince you, too.

Or even to strengthen your faith if you are already a Christian. I experienced this when I had thyroid cancer about ten years ago. I have fully recuperated, but of course living in the shadow of cancer, not knowing how things will turn out, is a traumatic experience. Once they tell you that you have cancer, even when they say you'll probably recover—well, it focuses the mind wonderfully on the meaning of life. I had a month of doing nothing and going nowhere while I was recovering. I was actually under quarantine because of all the radioactive iodine in my body, so I had nothing to do for the first time in probably thirty years (and probably the last time, too). So I sat down and read that 890-page book by N. T. Wright, including the footnotes, and it was astonishing. Of course I had believed in the resurrection before—I had staked my life and career on it. And of course I had the life, death, and resurrection of Jesus constantly at the front of my imagination. But what surprised me was the way this marshaling of evidence took my faith up a few notches. Before, I believed; but now, even more, I *believed*. Nowadays we are taught to think of faith as something that relates inversely to logic and evidence—as you get more facts and certainty, your need for faith goes down. But that's not what Christians mean by faith. Faith doesn't mean hoping in what isn't true; it means certainty about what you can't see. And so compelling evidence, evidence that engages rationality, is one of the greatest boosts to Christian faith.

There is in this passage another significant piece of evidence that these resurrection accounts are not made up. Who is the first eyewitness? John the Gospel writer tells us that the first eyewitness to the resurrection of Jesus Christ was Mary Magdalene, a woman. And all Bible experts and historians will tell you that in those times women could not testify in Jewish or

Roman courts. In those patriarchal cultures, a woman's testimony was considered unreliable and so inadmissible as evidence. This means that if you were fabricating an account of the resurrection in order to promote your religion or your movement, you would never make a woman the first eyewitness. And yet, in the accounts of Matthew, Mark, Luke, and John, the first eyewitnesses to the resurrection are women. The only historically plausible answer to why women are in the account at all—why the men who wrote these accounts would put women in when their testimony was considered unreliable—is because it must have happened. Mary must have been there. She must have seen Jesus Christ first. There's no other motive or reason for the author to say she was.

Faith has a significant rational component. Notice how the passage says, "Peter came along behind and went straight into the tomb. He saw the strips of linen lying there as well as the cloth that had been wrapped around Jesus' head. The cloth was lying still in its place separate from the linen." The word *saw* is actually the Greek word *blepo*, which means not just to see but to think, ponder, and process. Peter comes in, and he's probably thinking something like "If Jesus had revived and gotten up, the cloth would be all torn or unraveled. But if friends had taken the body, why in the world would they have dishonored the body by taking it away naked? They would have kept it in the grave clothes. But if enemies were doing it, why in the world would they have taken off the clothes and put them there nice and neat?" He's thinking hard, looking for evidence, testing all the possible hypotheses.

So faith is not only rational. You cannot get all the way to real faith through reasoning alone, yet faith is not *less than* rational either. You can't get to real faith without reason. Why? Because mature faith is an act of a whole person, so your intellect has to be committed as well as your will and emotions. We live in a time when people love to say, "There's really no objective truth. If you want to believe in Christianity, if you want to believe in whatever faith you want, if it's relevant for you, if it's satisfying to you—don't worry about if it actually happened. If it's relevant for you, you can believe it."

But passionate beliefs can be wrong. People passionately and sincerely have believed that their race was superior to all other races and that the best thing they could do was to rule the world. That didn't make them right. Why? Because down deep, we know there is such a thing as truth. We know that some things are wrong, even if people think they are right, and some things are right, even if people think they are wrong.

So true Christianity will never say, "Believe because it's relevant," or "Believe because it appeals to you." Christianity won't let you get away with that. It says, "Don't believe Christianity because it's exciting and practical and relevant—believe it because it's true. Because if it's not true, in the end it won't be practical and relevant." You can only face the suffering and questions ahead of you if you believe that Christianity's not just relevant and exciting (which it is!) but that it is also true.

So faith in Christ is impossible, and it is rational. There's one more thing to learn here. Faith comes by and in grace. In every way, faith is grace-filled. Let me explain.

> But Mary stood outside the tomb crying. As she wept, she bent over to look into the tomb and saw two angels in white, seated where Jesus' body had been, one at the head and the other at the foot.
>
> They asked her, "Woman, why are you crying?"
>
> "They have taken my Lord away," she said, "and I don't know where they have put him."
>
> At this, she turned around and saw Jesus standing there, but she did not realize that it was Jesus.
>
> "Woman," he said, "why are you crying? Who is it you are looking for?"
>
> Thinking he was the gardener, she said, "Sir, if you have carried him away, tell me where you have put him, and I will get him."
>
> Jesus said to her, "Mary."
>
> She turned toward him and cried out in Aramaic, "Rabboni!" [which means "Teacher"].
>
> Jesus said, "Do not hold on to me, for I have not yet ascended to the Father. Go instead to my broth-

ers and tell them, 'I am ascending to my Father and your Father, to my God and your God.' "

Mary Magdalene went to the disciples with the news: "I have seen the Lord!" And she told them that he had said these things to her. (John 20:11–18)

Here is perhaps the main point of the New Testament in narrative form.

At the outset, you can see the remarkable tenderness of this interaction. There are several places in the Old Testament where God confronts people who are seriously mistaken or wayward, doing so not with intimidating declarations but with gentle, probing questions. In the Garden of Eden, God asks disobedient Adam and Eve, "Where are you?" and "How did you come to feel shame?" To the rebellious prophet Jonah God asks, "Are you right to be angry?" Counselors know that it is not enough to simply tell people how to live. Asking questions helps the person to recognize their errors, to discover and embrace truth from their hearts. The questions of Jesus are similar. "Why are you crying?" is really a gentle rebuke to Mary, a call to wake up. "Who is it you are looking for?" is a more penetrating invitation to, as commentator D. A. Carson writes on this verse, "widen her horizons and to recognize that, grand as her devotion to him was, her estimate of him was still far too small."[14]

Notice, however, that Mary misinterprets Jesus' questions.

She thinks perhaps he is the caretaker of the place and that he might know where Jesus' body had been moved. So Jesus makes another effort to break through to her heart, and does so with a simple word. Earlier in this Gospel, Jesus said that he was the Good Shepherd, that he "calls his own sheep by name" and "his sheep follow him because they know his voice" (John 10:3–4). And that is what he does here, simply saying, "Mary." Real faith is always personal. If you only believe that Jesus died to forgive people *in general* for their sins—but you don't believe that Jesus died for *you*—you aren't taking hold of Jesus by faith. You haven't heard him call you by name.

The graciousness of Jesus is palpable. Mary is running around frantically but (as he hints) she's looking for the wrong Jesus. For a dead Jesus. For a Jesus infinitely less great than he really is. So she would never have found him unless he sought her. He comes to her, gently works to open her heart, and then breaks through with a personal address. Her faith comes by grace—she doesn't earn it.

But we learn even more here about the relationship of grace and faith. At the moment Mary realizes Jesus is alive, he sends her with the message "Go to my brothers and tell them . . ."—and in a sense she becomes the first Christian. Why? Well, what's a Christian? A Christian believes that Jesus died and was raised from the dead. A Christian has had an encounter with that risen Christ. And at this moment Mary is the only person in the world of whom those things are true.

Now, is this an accident? I don't believe so. Jesus could have easily arranged to make anyone the first messenger. He chose her. And that means Jesus Christ specifically chose a woman, not a man; chose a reformed mental patient, not a pillar of the community; chose one of the support team, not one of the leaders, to be the first Christian. How much clearer can he be? He is saying, "It doesn't matter who you are or what you've done. My salvation is not based on pedigree, it's not based on moral attainments, raw talent, level of effort, or track record. I have come not to call those who are strong, but to call those who are weak. And I am not mainly your teacher but your savior. I'm here to save you not by your work, but by my work." And the minute you understand that, the minute you see yourself in Mary Magdalene's place, something will change forever in you. You'll be following the first Christian.

You see, the text is not just telling us that grace is the *cause* of our faith, but it is the *content*, too. If you believe that Jesus was a great teacher and you believe he can help you and answer your prayers if you live according to his ethical prescriptions, you are not yet a Christian. That's general belief but not saving faith. Real Christian faith believes that Jesus saves us through his death and resurrection so we can be accepted by sheer grace. That is the gospel—the good news that we are saved by the work of Christ through grace.

Martin Luther talks about his own conversion experience.

He was a monk, a student and teacher of Scripture, and yet this is how he describes what happened:

> "In [the gospel] the righteousness of God is revealed [Romans 1:17]. . . . I hated that word 'righteousness of God.' . . . Though I lived as a monk without reproach, I felt that I was a sinner before God with an extremely disturbed conscience. I could not believe that he was placated by my satisfaction. . . . There I began to understand that the righteousness of God is that by which the righteous lives by a gift of God, namely by faith. . . . Here I felt that I was altogether born again and had entered paradise itself through open gates."[15]

This is how Luther came to understand that salvation is not a record I give God by which he saves me, but rather a record God gives me by which I am accepted and saved. He says, "The minute I understood that I felt myself to be reborn and gone through the open doors into paradise."

So faith is a gift of God. Built on thinking and evidence, activated by God's miraculous intervention, based on the radical discovery that Jesus has accomplished everything we need and we can be adopted and accepted into God's family, and all of this by sheer grace. Is that it? Do we simply sit down, content and transformed, with the knowledge of this love? No—we are to spend the rest of our lives tasting, experiencing, and being shaped by that gracious love. The end of the text gives us a tantalizing hint and picture of that experience.

Jesus says to Mary, "Do not hold on to me for I have not yet ascended to the Father." What's a bit puzzling is that when he meets Thomas later, he lets Thomas touch him. And when he meets the women at the end of the book of Matthew, he lets them touch him—they fall at his feet. So why does he say this to Mary? It's easy to imagine the exuberant Mary clutching at him for dear life, as if to say, "I lost you once. I'll never let you go again." If we understand that, then Jesus is saying, in effect, "You don't need to cling to me so tightly—I'm ascending." What is meant by this? Here's what many commentators say, and I think they're right. Jesus means: "Mary, when I ascend to the right hand of the Father I won't be leaving you at all. I will send my Spirit, and through the Spirit you can know my presence, peace, and love day or night." What a promise! Real faith connects you to Christ, not just for salvation from the penalty of your sins, but for an ongoing love relationship with him.

There's one last thing that is helpful to learn about faith from this passage. No two people come to faith in exactly the same way. If you read the whole chapter, you see that John, Peter, Mary, and Thomas (who meets Jesus later in Chapter 20) are all approached by Jesus differently. They need different amounts of time. They require different proportions of evidence and experience. They all have different trajectories, different paths. So you've got to be very careful not to say, "Well, my friend met Christ like that—so I have to have as dramatic an experience as he did." Or if you are the friend, you must not assume everyone else must come to faith in the same way you did. You have to admit you are a sinner. You have to believe he died in your place. You have to rest in his work rather than your own good works. You must commit your life to him in gratitude for his finished work. But there are so many pathways to this kind of faith.

I have always thought that when Mary Magdalene heard her own name on the lips of the risen Christ she must have felt as Annie Dillard did when she wrote, "I'd been my whole life a bell, but I never knew it until I was lifted up and rung."[16]

SIX

THE GREAT ENEMY

In the first five chapters, I have sought to address some of life's biggest questions using the life of Jesus as depicted in the New Testament Gospel of John. I've done that by looking at accounts of Jesus' encounters with everyday people, where we see that meeting Jesus changed their lives forever. But how can *we* encounter Christ today? In these case studies, we have seen again and again that Jesus does not primarily come as an example; his job is not to model for us the answers to the big questions. He's not even primarily a teacher, telling us the answers to those questions. No, he comes as a savior—to *be* the answer to the big questions. To do for us what we could not hope to do on our own.

If we want our lives to be changed forever, we, too, need to encounter him as a savior. To do that we need to see what he did for us. And it is in the key events of Jesus' life, where we can see most clearly *how* he becomes a savior for us. So in these final five chapters, I will look at some of these pivotal events in the life of Jesus as they are presented in the New Testament Gospels.

(You may wonder why I've left out the three best-known events of Jesus' life—his birth, death, and resurrection. The reason is that because these events are more familiar to us, their meanings for us are generally clearer. Without the incarnation, for example, Jesus could not have become human and taken our punishment. The crucifixion means that there's a solution for guilt, a pardon for sin. The resurrection means we will eventually get new bodies that will signal our triumph over death. All of these great and miraculous events of Jesus' life are obviously crucial and we have looked at each of them to some degree in the earlier chapters. In the following pages, we will look at some less well-known incidents that take us even deeper into what Jesus did to save us. He overcomes evil for us [chapter 6], intercedes for us [chapter 7], obeys perfectly for us [chapter 8], leaves earth to reign for us [chapter 9], and leaves heaven to die for us [chapter 10].)

Let's look first at how Jesus' public life was launched. Two events happened back-to-back to prepare him for the single most world-changing career in history. In three of the four Gospels, these incidents—Jesus' baptism and his subsequent temptation by Satan in the desert—are presented together, and I believe this is for a good reason.

Here is the story from Matthew, chapters 3 and 4:

Then Jesus came from Galilee to the Jordan to be baptized by John. But John tried to deter him, saying, "I need to be baptized by you, and do you come to me?" Jesus replied, "Let it be so now; it is proper for us to do this to fulfill all righteousness." Then John consented. As soon as Jesus was baptized, he went up out of the water. At that moment heaven was open, and he saw the Spirit of God descending like a dove and alighting on him. And a voice from heaven said, "This is my Son, whom I love; with him I am well pleased."

Then Jesus was led by the Spirit into the wilderness to be tempted by the devil. After fasting forty days and forty nights, he was hungry. The tempter came and said, "If you are the Son of God, tell these stones to become bread." Jesus answered, "It is written: 'Man shall not live on bread alone, but on every word that comes from the mouth of God.'" Then the devil took him to the holy city and had him stand on the highest point of the temple. "If you are the Son of God," he said, "throw yourself down. For it is written: 'He will command his angels concerning you, and they will lift you up in their hands, so that you will not strike your foot against the stone.'" Jesus answered him, "It is also written: 'Do not put the Lord your God to the test.'" Again, the devil took him to a very high mountain and showed him all the kingdoms of the world and their splendor. "All of this I will give you," he said, "if you bow down and worship me." Jesus said to him, "Away from me, Satan! For it is written: 'Worship the Lord your God, and serve him only.'" And the devil left him. (Matthew 3:13–4:11)

Outside of the crucifixion itself, the baptism is the only event of Jesus' life mentioned in all four Gospels. It is crucial. But only here in Matthew is the temptation scene recorded in detail. And it is important to recognize how the baptism and temptation are connected tightly by the single word *then*. God spoke words of powerful assurance: "This is my Son, whom I love; with him I am well pleased." *Then* Jesus was led by the Spirit into the desert to be tempted by the devil. *Then* is almost *therefore*. After great blessing and success came trial and temptation.

No one can ever seem to secure a life of sustained success, joy, and blessing. As hard as we try, no matter what precautions we take, no matter how well things are going, something comes in to ruin it. Even the most talented, diligent, and savvy people can't escape the undulations of life. "Ah," you may say, "but what if we did our part better? What if we lived good lives and obeyed God and prayed every day, asking him to protect us from all suffering and difficulty?" The answer is, fine—go there. What if you actually could overcome *all* of your faults and flaws? What if you could become perfectly wise and understand God's ways, the human heart, and the times and seasons—such that you always made wise decisions? What if you could have faith in God without wavering? What if your life were perfectly pleasing to God? Then—surely! God would protect you, and your own holiness and wisdom would guard you as well, and your life would always go well. Right?

Wrong. Because here stands the one who did it. God the Father has just said that Jesus' life is perfectly pleasing to him. And the Spirit of God has descended on him to guide him. And look what happens. He is loved and affirmed and empowered by God, and then . . . *then!* He is ushered into the clutches of the devil. So here's the order: God's love and power, then evil, temptation, wilderness, terrible hunger and thirst. That little word *then* is an amazing word. It is almost like Matthew is trying to tell us, "Read my lips: No one is exempt from trials and tribulations. In fact, this is often what happens to people God loves very much, for it is part of God's often mysterious and good plan for turning us into something great."

This all goes to tell us, by the way, that Job's friends were wrong. You may remember that in the book of Job, Job seemed to be living an exemplary life, and then virtually everything in his life that could go wrong did go wrong. He lost his family, all of his considerable fortune, and his health. He was sent, as it were, into the wilderness. Job's friends came to see him, saw what was happening, and essentially said this: "Look, Job. Our lives are the product of our choices. If you choose to live right and well, your life will *go* right and well. If God loved you, he wouldn't let such things happen. He must be mad at you and the choices you've made."

This is how many people think—maybe even most people. When people who are middle-class look at the poor, they assume the poor just aren't working as hard as they are. When people in healthy families look at people with struggling and dysfunctional ones, they assume they haven't cared enough to do things right. If we are not suffering at the moment, there is a tendency for us to take credit for it in our minds. It's not luck or grace—it's because we are living good and smart lives. Right? But in Matthew 3 we see the one person in the history of the world who really *did* live a good life, even a perfect life, and merited the full love of God. He actually earned a pass from suffering and inconvenience. Yet his life went terribly! And this temptation scene is just the start, just the opening round. There will be a steady progression of rejection, attempts on his life, betrayal, poverty, grief, loss, torture, and finally death. He will be tried and executed in an act of injustice. Everything will go wrong for Jesus from this point.

What does this show us? One thing it demonstrates is the power, complexity, and intractability of evil in the world. Secular people see the world as made up of strictly material forces.

There is no soul or spirit, no demons or angels. Everything has a natural scientific explanation. In this view, we can deal with evil in the world (if there even is such a thing) by educating the ignorant, changing the social systems, and providing better psychological and pharmacological treatment. Yet time and again over the last century, Western thinkers have been shocked anew by the depth and power of the forces of evil in the human heart and in the world. Columbia professor Andrew Delbanco, in his book *The Death of Satan: How Americans Have Lost the Sense of Evil*, writes, "A gulf has opened up in our culture between the visibility of evil and the intellectual resources available for coping with it."

But the Bible can bridge that gulf and account for all that we experience personally and witness in the sweep of history. It says that evil is more multidimensional, nuanced, and complex than the sciences alone can suggest. It maintains that, in addition to systemic injustices and personal ignorance and physiological imbalances, there really are forces of spiritual evil in the world—and behind them all, there is a singular supernatural intelligence. The Western world has largely rejected this dimension of evil that the Bible gives us, and as a result, we, like Job's friends, are always underestimating—and sometimes misdiagnosing—the power of evil in our lives. For example, deep down we cling to the simplistic idea that if we are good, life will go well. Yet if there are demonic forces, it stands to reason that true goodness and godliness would actually attract and stir up those powers to attack. And that is just what we see here in the baptism and temptation account.

(To believe that moral goodness will result in a good life is also a simplistic understanding of God's purposes for us. He is infinitely wise, can see the end from the beginning, and has good purposes for us hidden on the far side of the wilderness.[17] Just as Job's patience in suffering turned him into an example that has helped hundreds of millions of people, and just as Jesus' temptations prepared him for his history-changing and world-saving career, so God's Spirit leads us into our wildernesses for our good.)

We're constantly being shocked, then, by the intractability of evil in the world, but this is partially because we moderns see the Bible as "primitive" and do not listen to its account of reality. But if the Bible is right, and this kind of evil exists, what good does it do us to understand more about it? Well, when the Bible speaks about our encounters with supernatural evil in life, it uses battle language. And if you don't know where the attack is going to come from, or if you underestimate or mischaracterize the enemy, you're likely to lose the battle. So if we do know what's out there and where it's coming from, how do we face it without being overwhelmed? Let's consider what the text of Matthew 3 indicates. It tells us that to face true evil we need to answer three questions: Who is the enemy? Where is the front? What is our best defense in this fight?

First, who is the enemy? As we have been saying, the biblical view of evil is that it is complex and comprehensive. You can't confine it to human choices, or in social systems, or in psychological problems, or in a simple lack of education—in fact, you can't even locate it fully within this whole set of forces taken together. Nor can you take the scapegoating views that have wreaked so much havoc in history—namely that evil is mainly caused by *those* people over there. "Those people" may be of a certain race, class, nation, religion, or political ideology. The Bible says that evil is both natural *and* supernatural, that evil is both inside of us *and* outside of us, that evil is both individual *and* socially systemic. There's no human way to get fully away from it or even get to the bottom of it in our understanding.

Historically there have been two main rivals to the biblical view that try to explain the nature of evil. On one end you have *dualism*, which says there are equal and opposite forces of evil and good in the world. Reality fundamentally rests upon the clash between these two forces, which will go on battling until the end of time, or even eternally. That means that there's absolutely no triumph possible. In this view, God is not really any more powerful than Satan. Augustine, in *The City of God,* pointed out that paganism is dualistic. Most forms of paganism say that there are good gods and bad gods, good powers and bad powers. This means, however, that the world is fundamentally and irremediably a violent place, not a place of order and beauty and hope. It consists of multiple power centers that are forever at war with one another. You can perhaps create an island of peace and order, but eventually something will overrun it. There's really no hope in the end for any way to resolve the struggle and bring lasting peace.

The other philosophical approach to evil is *monism*, or pantheism. This view goes to the other extreme and claims that all reality is One. Everything is part of God, God is everything, and therefore everything is ultimately one with everything else. Individual selves, in this view, are something of an illusion. We are all connected in a deep way—not just connected by a shared experience of humanity but actually, in the end, indistinct from one another. C. S. Lewis says in *Mere Christianity* that the pantheist can look at a person dying of cancer or extreme poverty and say, "If you could only see it from the divine point of view, you would realize that this also is God." Evil and suffering, then, are not eternal and undefeatable, as in dualism. They don't even really exist—so we could say they are an illusion.

It is interesting to observe that modern secular culture regards evil in a rather fragmented, incoherent way, borrowing from both of these views. On one hand, secularism is like ancient polytheism in that it sees the world as not created by a single, all-powerful Artist but as the product of violent and uncontrolled forces. Not only is the physical universe itself the product of an unending series of explosions and combustions, but we ourselves are only the products of evolution, of the survival of the fittest. If this account of the world is correct, then violence has no cure—it is the fabric of all reality. We got here through violent and purposeless means, and we will continue to exist and evolve in the same way. At the same time, many secular thinkers view human evil as the product of either bad social systems or psychological conditions. In the nineteenth century, secular thinkers began to propose that if you're a serial killer, it's because you were the product of bad parenting, or of poverty, or of some other kind of deprivation. That is, something had to have happened to you for you to do something like murder another person, because human beings are not inherently evil. More contemporary secular thought is relativistic. What looks evil from a certain cultural perspective, it is said, goes away when looked at from another perspective. One man's terrorist is another man's freedom fighter. So—evil is all in the eye of the beholder. If you look at it differently, it goes away. It is an illusion.

In Delbanco's book *The Death of Satan: How Americans Have Lost the Sense of Evil* he quotes from Thomas Harris's novel *The Silence of the Lambs,* where the monstrous killer Hannibal Lecter is talking to Officer Starling. He's describing the bad things he's done, and she looks at him and says, "What happened to you that you could do this? Who did something to you that you could be so bad?" And he looks at her and says:

> "Nothing happened to me, Officer Starling. *I* happened. You can't reduce me to a set of influences.

You've given up good and evil for behaviorism, Officer Starling. You've got everybody in moral dignity pants—nothing is ever anybody's fault. Look at me, Officer Starling. Can you stand to say I'm evil?"[18]

Delbanco goes on to say that these words are the epitome of modern horror—our generation's growing awareness that we cannot answer the monster's question. He says, if you get rid of the idea of sin, Satan, and cosmic evil, then every bad deed has solely psychological or sociological roots. And that trivializes the suffering of the victims and the magnitude of what's happened. Hannibal Lecter knows Officer Starling is the result of modern secular thinking, and so he knows he's got her. He asks a question her worldview doesn't have the resources to answer. He says in effect, "You have to tell all the families of those poor people that I beheaded and ate that my mother didn't love me. You can't hold me responsible. You can't even hold *her* responsible." He has the modern world right where he wants it.

At the end of the first Harry Potter book, J. K. Rowling has a puppet of the Dark Lord Voldemort say, "Lord Voldemort showed me . . . there is no good and evil, there is only power."[19] I think Rowling is saying there may be few things more evil than denying that there's evil. That's what Satan wants.

You may find it interesting that Christianity gives you neither dualism nor monism. Instead, it gives you something you may see as slightly more plausible than you did before: an actual devil. If it's true that there are demonic forces out there, then the evil in the world cannot be reduced simply to human choices. Don't get me wrong—human beings all by themselves are capable of great sin, and of course those sinful human choices are a significant component of the matrix of evil in the world. But when I moved to a small town in the South in the 1970s, I could see the tail end of the society and the institutions that had kept African Americans excluded from any economic or political power. If you talked to the individuals in those institutions, while many of them were definitely bigots, and even more were merely clueless, you realized that most of the individuals were not especially evil in themselves. Yet the systems they comprised were certainly evil. Remember that Hannah Arendt saw this when she covered the trial of the Nazi death camp leader Adolf Eichmann for *The New Yorker*, and spoke there of the "banality of evil." The system was far more evil and destructive than the thousands of fairly ordinary individuals who made it up. There's some kind of force out there that magnifies, complicates, and perpetuates the bad things that are happening in the social and psychological systems of the world. Christianity says there's more evil than you can account for in the world just from the cumulative effect of wrong individual choices. And you can attribute some of that evil to actual demonic forces.

But on the other hand, Christianity is not dualistic. The demonic forces are not the equal of God. The devil is a fallen angel leading fallen angels, and God is infinitely more powerful. And in the very end, not only *can* God overcome them all, but he certainly *will*. That is the electrifying promise and hope that blows through all the pages of the Bible.

Maybe you think that the idea of the devil is a primitive idea, a belief for simple people. I have been arguing—and I would respectfully suggest—that if you are trying to explain the world without the existence of the devil, it is you who are being spiritually and intellectually naive.

Now, let's get more practical. If we know who the enemy is, the second question to consider is, Where is the front? What does the Scripture tell us besides the fact that there is a devil? It tells us where the main front is, the main point of attack. Notice that several times the devil says, "If you are the Son of God. . . ." That is his main attack, not only against Jesus but against us as well. God has just assured Jesus that he is God's beloved Son, and Satan immediately and directly assaults Jesus at that very spot. He asks Jesus, essentially, to make God prove that he loves him and empowers him. But you don't need to ask someone for demonstrations and assurances and proofs unless you doubt. And that's Satan's main military goal—he wants Jesus to lose the certainty, the assurance of God's full acceptance, of his unconditional fatherly love.

Now, if that is Satan's main front of attack, how does he

seek to accomplish this with us? To begin with, he wants to keep you from believing Jesus is really the Son of God and Savior of the world. Notice carefully what God said from heaven in the baptism. First he says, "This is my Son, whom I love"—a quote from Psalm 2, a song about God's messianic king who is going to put down all rebellion and evil in the world. But then God says, "with him I am well pleased." That is a quote from Isaiah 53, where it describes the figure of the Suffering Servant, a mysterious person who Isaiah says will someday suffer and die for the transgressions of the people. This is an important key to understanding the whole Bible. Throughout the Old Testament (as in Psalm 2) we find the promise of a great messianic king who would come and put everything right in the world. Many of the Jews awaited him eagerly. But there was also this suffering figure in the prophecy of Isaiah. The Jews were told that this servant would be rejected, that "by his wounds we [would be] healed" (Isaiah 53:5). And no one, until God blessed Jesus at the baptism, had put those two people together.

God was trying to get us to understand this: Jesus is not just a good man who by word and example tells us how to live. Nor is he merely a heavenly king who came to destroy all evil in one stroke. As we have seen, evil is deep within us. And if he had come to end all evil on the spot, he would have ended us. Instead, he is a king who comes not to a throne but to a cross. He comes to be tempted and tried, to suffer and die. Why? So that we can receive God's love as a gift. As the hymn goes: "Before the throne absolved we stand; / Your love has met your law's demand."[20]

And so, if we rest in Christ's work for us, we can be adopted into God's family by grace (John 1:12). It means that we can know that *we* are also God's beloved children, and that—in Christ—we are well pleasing. That assurance is the taproot of the deepest, most life-giving joy possible. On one hand it means we now *want* to turn away from any sin or thing that displeases our Father. We no longer do so out of fear of punishment or out of need to prove ourselves. Those motives are exhausting and inevitably create narrowness, self-righteousness, and hardness of heart. No. Instead, out of grateful joy and sheer desire to resemble, delight, and serve the one who saved us, we amend our lives with a new effectiveness. And on the other hand, the fears and anxieties and insecurities that haunted us begin to dissipate. Success and failure in our work neither puffs us up nor devastates us. We are not driven by unhappiness over our looks, or our status—we are not deflated by criticism as we were before. Our self-image rests in a love we can't lose.

Do you see why Satan would make this the main front of his attack? Satan wants at all cost to stop people from ever acquiring this kind of power. For people who don't believe Christianity, he aims to keep them blind to who Jesus really is. He wants them to believe that Jesus is an especially nice man. For people who think they believe Christianity but don't understand that salvation is a free gift through Christ, Satan hopes to keep them ignorant of the gospel itself. He wants them confused about the fact that we are justified—put right with God—by faith in Christ alone, not by our moral efforts.

But for those of us who know in principle that we are adopted, loved sons and daughters, Satan wants us to slide back into a self-image based on our moral performance, our goodness and efforts. This happened to a former minister I spoke with years ago. While he preached what you and I would call orthodox Christian sermons, deep in his heart Satan had defeated him. With his head and mouth he said, "We are saved by Jesus and by grace." But his heart was operating on a very different narrative. If the language of his heart could have been made audible, it would have sounded something like this: "Here's how I'm going to be sure I'm a good and worthy person. I'm going to be a minister. There's nobody better than that. A minister! Telling people about the truth. Helping suffering people. Helping people put their lives together." In other words, while his head said that Jesus was his Savior, he was seeking to be his own savior.

As a result, when his church was growing, his ministry was going well, and his preaching was in demand, he slowly but surely began to become cold, smug, and superior. His preaching became more caustic, and he became more imperious and critical in his interactions with people. This led to several conflicts with key families, who as a result left the church. And when the church started to do poorly, he couldn't take it. It wasn't just a loss of the people—it was a loss of his identity. He began to drink to deal with the pain. And he had an affair with a woman who gave him the adulation he craved. His marriage and ministry collapsed.

What happened? Satan, of course, had won. If you think of your heart's identity as an engine, you could say there is a kind of fuel that powers it cleanly and efficiently—and a kind of fuel that is not only polluting but also destroys the engine. The dirty fuel is the fuel of fear and the need to prove yourself. Or the need to be needed by someone else. Or the need to express yourself fully and without restraint. There are many "fuels" that motivate us to live for a time—but only one fuel is clean and will not lead to weariness and disappointment. And that is God's love for you. Any other fuel will become demonic. It will obsess you or at best merely let you down. Whenever you're running your life on those fuels, Satan's got you where he wants you. The one thing he does not want is that God's words "You are my beloved child" power the engine of your life and heart.

J. C. Ryle was the Anglican bishop of Liverpool, England, in the late nineteenth century. In an essay titled "Assurance," he writes very movingly about this effect:

> Now assurance goes far to set a child of God free. . . . It enables him to feel that the great busi-

ness of life is a settled business, the great debt a paid debt, the great disease a healed disease, and the great work a finished work; and all other business, diseases, debts, and works, are then by comparison small. In this way assurance makes him patient in tribulation, calm under bereavements, unmoved in sorrow, not afraid of evil tidings; in every condition content, for it gives him a FIXEDNESS of heart. It sweetens his bitter cups, it lessens the burden of his crosses, it smoothes the rough places over which he travels, and it lightens the valley of the shadow of death. It makes him always feel that he has something solid beneath his feet, and something firm under his hands—a sure friend by the way, and a sure home at the end. . . . There is a beautiful expression in the Prayer-book service for the Visitation of the Sick: "The Almighty Lord, who is a most strong tower to all them that put their trust in Him, be now and evermore thy defence, and make thee *know* and *feel* that there is none other name under heaven, through whom thou mayest receive health and salvation, but only the name of our Lord Jesus Christ."[21]

What is our best defense in this fight? Again, let's see what we can learn from the text. First we see that Jesus does not deal with Satan in what I'll call a superstitious, magical way. He doesn't simply blast him with his glory. I'm not saying that there is no such thing as demon possession that merits a word of command. Obviously in the Gospels we do see Jesus doing this in certain cases. But in general, Satan doesn't control us with fang marks on the flesh, but with lies in the heart. We see this in the Garden of Eden account, where Satan tempts Adam and Eve. He doesn't come in with all sorts of special effects; he suggests ideas to the heart that contradict God's word, impugn his character, and destroy the trust relationship we have with him. The same should be true with us. Our best defense in the fight against the influence of Satan's lies is generally not the production of incantations but the rehearsal of truth.

Notice the way Jesus uses the Bible. That is one of the most obvious messages of the passage. Jesus uses the Scripture *every time* he is assaulted by the devil. That strategy, of course, fits in with what we have just said about the front of battle. Satan wants to destroy our grasp on the truth. But even more, he wants to affect the beliefs of our heart. According to the Bible, the heart is not just the seat of the emotions but also the source of our fundamental commitments, hopes, and trust. And from the heart flow our thinking, feelings, and actions. What the heart trusts, the mind justifies, the emotions desire, and the will carries out. If Satan can get you to consent with your mind to a God of loving grace but get your heart to believe that you must do X, Y, and Z in order to be a worthy, lovable, and valuable person, he will be most satisfied.

This is why everything Satan says that insinuates or openly denies the promises and revelation of God is answered with Scripture itself. Jesus quotes Deuteronomy 8:3, then 6:16, and finally 6:13. Even as he was dying on the cross, when he was in his deepest agony, he quoted Psalm 22:1: "My God, my God, why have you forsaken me?" When you are in moments of pain or shock, the things that come out of your mind and mouth are the most primal things in your being. And when Jesus was in such moments, out came the words of the Bible. Something like 10 percent of all the things he says in the Bible are quotations of, or allusions to, the Hebrew Scriptures. When you know Scripture that well, you process all thoughts and feelings through a grid of biblical revelation. And when you have God's own assurances, summonses, promises, and revelations secured that deep inside you, it's extremely difficult for Satan to get a foothold and block your assurance of your salvation. You aren't vulnerable along the front where he can best attack you.

Now I have to ask you: If Jesus Christ, the Son of God, did not presume to face the forces of evil in the world without a profound knowledge of the Bible in mind and heart, how could we try to face life any other way? It's true that this takes a great deal of time and effort. Worship, daily reading, meditation and memorization, singing, listening to teaching—all of these are necessary to become as acquainted with the Scripture as we must be. And when we are under attack—tempted to sin, or to be discouraged, or to just give up altogether—it is then that we must wrestle the words and promises of the Bible into the center of our being, to "let the message of Christ dwell among you richly" (Colossians 3:16). It will feel very much like a fight indeed. J. C. Ryle wrote:

> True Christianity is a fight. . . . There is a vast quantity of religion current in the world which is not true, genuine Christianity. It passes muster; it satisfies sleepy consciences; but it is not good money. . . . There are thousands of men and women who go to churches every Sunday . . . but you never see any "fight" about their religion! Of spiritual strife, and exertion, and conflict, and self-denial, and watching, and warring they know literally nothing at all.[22]

Please do not disconnect the temptation and the baptism. Satan comes to Jesus because Jesus has been *commissioned*—empowered by God for a mission. He is shortly about to embark on an intense period of teaching and healing and liberating people from spiritual bondage. Like Jesus, we battle with Satan not merely in our hearts but out in the world when we seek to undo his work. When we seek to help a person find faith in Christ, or when we love our poor neighbor through deeds of compassion and service, we are fighting him on that front, too. When C. S. Lewis wrote about the pantheist's belief that suffering is an illusion, he went on to insist that Christians cannot indulge in such passivity in the face of evil.

> Confronted with a cancer or a slum the Pantheist can say, "If you could only see it from the divine point of view, you would realise that this also is God." The Christian replies, "Don't talk damned nonsense." For Christianity is a fighting religion. It thinks God made the world—that space and time, heat and cold, and all the colours and tastes, and all the animals and vegetables, are things that God "made up out of His head" as a man makes up a story. But it also thinks that a great many things have gone wrong with the world that God made and that God insists, and insists very loudly, on our putting them right again.[23]

We have one more resource for this spiritual warfare. And it is right before us in this passage—it is Jesus himself. Hebrews 4:15 tells us he is our great high priest. Priests were counselors and healers, and we are told that Jesus can "empathize with our weaknesses" and can give us "mercy and . . . grace to help us in our time of need" (Hebrews 4:16). Why? Because he was "tempted in every way, just as we are—yet he did not sin" (v. 15). He is there to help us face the reality of evil, both inside and outside ourselves, having done it himself as a man. So as we fight Satan's lies in our hearts, and his works in our world, let's rely not only on the Word of the Lord, but also on the Lord of the Word. We don't simply have a book, as perfect as it is—we have Jesus himself, who has been through fiery trials so intense that we can't imagine them. And he has done it all for us. Now, strengthened with his deep empathy and tender power, we can come through it all at his side.

SEVEN

THE TWO ADVOCATES

When we think of Jesus' last evening with his disciples, we normally think of the Last Supper in that upper room where they celebrated Passover. While Matthew, Mark, and Luke tell us a great deal about the Supper, the Gospel of John never mentions the breaking of bread or the drinking of wine—it doesn't talk about the meal at all. Yet John gives us more information than anyone else about what happened in that room on that night. John provides us with what has been called Jesus' Farewell Discourse, a long three-chapter address followed by a majestic prayer that takes up another chapter. Now, when you are about to die, you don't beat around the bush, and you don't go on tangents. You say the things that are most pressing on your mind and most important to your listeners. Knowing that, we should give great weight to Jesus' main theme in this passage. While he touches on many subjects and topics, there seems to be one theme that is most prominent. It weighs on his heart just before his death. What is it?

Over the previous three years, the apostles had an ongoing personal encounter with Jesus Christ. They lived and worked with him, they talked and prayed with him. But now Jesus said, "My children, I will be with you only a little longer. . . . Where I am going, you cannot come" (John 13:33). This statement touches off expressions of alarm. Peter claims that he certainly *will* follow Jesus, wherever he goes, even at the cost of his life (13:37). Thomas is more circumspect but still confused, saying that since they don't really know what he is talking about, where exactly is he going; how can they come? (14:5). When Jesus responds that he is going to his "Father's house" (14:2–3), Philip asks that Jesus would "show us the Father" (14:8).

Now, if you have been reading the full account of Jesus' life and ministry with these men, you will see how clueless such statements really are. Peter has no self-knowledge at all. "Will you really lay down your life for me?" Jesus asks him (13:38). But even more, despite Jesus' constant teaching that he was to die for people's sins, it simply has not sunk in. Jesus plaintively asks, "Don't you know me . . . even after I have been among you such a long time?" (14:9). That is a cutting question revealing a terrible fact. After all this time and attention, Jesus says, "You don't really know me. You haven't really had the deep, personal encounter with me that you need." The apostles have little understanding of their own hearts or, worse, of Jesus' heart and purposes.

So the situation is dire. These are Jesus' handpicked agents to take his message to the world. Yet they don't really know him, and the following day he will die! Not only that, but Jesus knows they are in for a great deal of persecution and opposition, beginning at the cross. What hope now is there that they will ever know him and carry his message forward? But there is hope—and Jesus unveils it at first in an enigmatic way. He says to them:

> I will ask the Father, and he will give you another advocate to help you and be with you forever—the Spirit of truth. The world cannot accept him, because it neither sees him nor knows him. But you know him, for he lives with you and will be in you. I will not leave you as orphans; I will come to you. Before long, the world will not see me anymore, but you will see me. Because I live, you also will live. On that day you will realize that I am in my Father, and you are in me, and I am in you. . . . All this I have spoken while still with you. But the Advocate, the Holy Spirit, whom the Father will send in my name, will teach you all things and will remind you of everything I have said to you. Peace I leave with you; my peace I give to you. I do not give to you as the

world gives. Do not let your hearts be troubled or afraid. (John 14:16–20; 25–27)

Here Jesus says several remarkable things. He is talking about God's Spirit coming to the disciples, and anyone who has read the Hebrew Scriptures knows that the Spirit of God is a force in the world that proceeds from the Father. But Jesus speaks of the Spirit in certain ways that would have been extraordinary to them.

First, he says that the Spirit is not merely a force, but a person. In Greek, nouns are assigned a gender—masculine, feminine, or neutral—and the Greek word for "spirit" is *neuter*. But Jesus here often speaks of the Spirit as "he"—showing that he is not speaking of some nebulous divine energy. Jesus is saying that after he leaves—after he dies—the Father will send a person in his place. Second, Jesus says that he will be leaving and this person will be coming. "Unless I go away, the Advocate will not come; but if I go, I will send him to you" (John 16:7). And yet, in some other sense, he says "*I* will come to you" (John 14:18). It is somehow through this person that they will be able to "see" Jesus even though the world will not, because he will not be present bodily. In one sense he will be gone, but in another sense his presence will remain, mediated by this person the Father is sending.

So who is this person? Jesus calls this person "another Advocate." This name is different in nearly every translation. The old King James Version calls him "Comforter," while other translations render it "Helper" or "Counselor." Whenever you find that translations disagree like this, it's usually because the original word's meaning is too nuanced and rich to convey via a single English word. A "comforter" can make you think of mere hand-holding, a "counselor" of just listening, while a "helper" might make you think of a child or a relatively un-skilled assistant. This may be one of the reasons why the New International Version uses the term *Advocate*, a legal word, sometimes used for an attorney who represents you in court. And this translation brings out different aspects of this rich word.

The Greek word in this case is the word *paraklete*. *Paraklete* is a noun, the verb form being *parakaleo*. *Kaleo* means to call or direct someone. *Para* means to come alongside, the prefix appearing often with the same meaning in English, as in *paralegal* or *paramedic*. It means to come alongside in order to support. Now, perhaps you notice some tension here. To call someone is forceful. It is active, not passive. You are point-ing him or her toward a truth or toward a goal. You aren't just talking, or even asking—you are pressing toward something. And yet to "come alongside" means to be sympathetic, to be in a relationship, to stand in someone's shoes. This word is a union of prophetic challenge and priestly support.

That's why the word *counselor* is actually not so bad, if we think about it in a particular sense. When you and I think of that word in our time, we almost immediately think of a therapist. But this term would be better understood when we think of "a counselor at law," a defense attorney. Your defense attorney is sympathetically on and at your side, to be sure. But he or she is not there merely to comfort you. Indeed, your defense lawyer may have hard and challenging things to say to you, yet always in order to help your case and cause. And he or she does not merely speak to you—but also speaks to the powers that be *for* you. This is why the translations that call the Holy Spirit the Advocate are also, I believe, on the right track.

That's how God's Spirit is defined, or described, in the word Jesus uses to talk about him. But we must notice also that Jesus calls the Spirit *another* Advocate or counselor. Who, then, is the first Advocate? The only other place in the New Testament where the word *paraklete* is used is in 1 John 2:1–2: "If anyone does sin, we have an advocate [*paraklete*] with the Father—Jesus Christ, the Righteous One. He is the atoning sacrifice for our sins." So Jesus is the first Advocate, and the Spirit is the second.

And I want you to know that in this word—*advocate, counselor*—we have the key to understanding not only Jesus' work on the cross but also the Sprit's work in our hearts. Indeed, I'd argue that unless you know that Jesus was the first Advocate, you won't understand the work of the Holy Spirit as the second Advocate at all. This is the solution to the problem Jesus saw in the upper room that night—men who after three years of instruction and intimacy still did not understand his work or know him deeply. Let's look first at what this word shows us about Jesus' work, and then about the Spirit's work.

What did Jesus do on the cross? You may say, "That's easy. He died for our sins and that means we can be forgiven." But Jesus, by calling himself our Advocate in the upper room, is showing us that his death was a more radical act than that. The first thing the term implies is that there is a bar of justice somewhere—a kind of universal, divine court before which we all stand. Now, some of you are saying, "I'm a sophisticated person here; I'm skeptical about this idea of a divine judgment." But give me a moment to show you why I think, down deep, you may sense that this judgment is really there after all.

To me one of the most terrifying scenes in all of literature is in Arthur Miller's play *Death of a Salesman*. Willy Loman is a traveling salesman who feels that he is largely a failure. His self-pity leads him to regularly cheat on his wife in his travels. He rationalizes as men do—"I have a hard life" or "the affairs don't mean anything"—and so on.

Perhaps his only consolation in life is that his son Biff idolizes him, but one day Biff shows up at his hotel room and catches him with a woman, and it's an excruciating scene. At first, Willy tries to swagger and he says, "Now look, Biff, when you grow up you'll understand about these things." And Biff just stares at him. And then Willy tries to bully his son and tells him to forget the whole incident, saying, "That's an order!"

But when Biff finally runs away, calling him a liar and a "phony little fake," Willy falls on his knees, his soul stripped naked of all his rationalizations. When I read that scene, I just shiver. All of his excuses simply melt away before Biff's guileless, innocent eyes that can finally see things as they really are. Willy sputters and spins—but his cynicism and self-deceptions and false justifications fall away and he is left there, soul-naked, before those honest eyes.

Now, at one place in the second chapter of Paul's letter to the Romans, he says that deep down all people have a sense (though they may repress it) that somewhere there is a divine set of eyes looking at us like that. But these eyes are infinitely more penetrating, fair, and honest than Biff's. And when we come before those eyes, all of our excuses are going to dissolve away. Of course there are plenty of people who say, "I don't believe that there's such a thing as divine justice. I believe that right and wrong are relative to people and cultures." But isn't it true that the very next minute, you act as if there is such a thing as justice? If you see someone being ruthless with you— though not doing anything illegal—don't you feel that whatever they may believe about what they are doing, it is just *wrong*? You don't think to yourself, "According to my moral feelings this is wrong, but according to his it may not be." No, you instinctively know that there are things that are wrong even if their culture or their family or their feelings condone it. Even if it feels natural to them, we know nonetheless it's not the way things are supposed to be. And what's natural can be wrong only if there is a "super-natural" standard by which you could judge it. We can't escape the fact that we know there is a bar of justice somewhere for all of us.

This is what the Bible teaches, that we all stand judged. There *is* a standard for our lives that we must all deal with. And here is our dilemma. If the Bible is wrong and there is no God, if there is no bar of justice, and violence and injustice are just natural, then what hope is there for the world? But if there *is* a bar of justice, then what hope is there for you and me? No one lives up to even his or her own moral standards, let alone God's. Look at the Golden Rule: Do unto others as you would have them do unto you. Everybody agrees to that rule, and yet who's actually keeping it?

What do you think the conscience is? According to Paul in Romans 2, the conscience is like a radio receiver picking up transmissions from that seat of justice. You think, "Oh, the reason I always feel guilty is because of my mother. She did this to me." So you've gotten a lot of therapy but you still feel guilty—why is that? Well, a poor family background may twist your conscience so it overreacts to some things and under-reacts to others—but your family couldn't create that sense of guilt; it can only aggravate it. Paul writes that those who don't know or believe God's law nonetheless "show that the require-ments of the law are written on their hearts, their consciences also bearing witness, and their thoughts sometimes accusing them." (Romans 2:15). So if this divine judgment exists, it is not merely a problem for us later; it's a problem for us *now*. We give it names that allow us to blame others for it—"lack of self-esteem" or "shame and guilt"—but really it's that bar of justice that even healthy consciences are channeling into our lives, our emotions, our self-understanding, every minute we're awake. Even when we clear away overbearing parents and oppressive cultural norms—even when we are left with our own freely chosen moral standards—we still feel accused. There's a voice within that tells us we are fools, we are imposters, we are failures, and we are not what we should be.

So deep down we know that this bar of justice is there, just as the Bible tells us it is. And we know we are in no condition to stand before it alone. When the Bible says Jesus is an advocate, it assumes the existence of that bar of justice and the fact that we must deal with it, must stand before it. That's the first thing this word *advocate* implies.

The second thing it implies is that Jesus Christ is not primarily an example of moral behavior (though he is), nor primarily a loving supporter (though he is that, too). Those things would be helpful, but on their own they would fall short of what we need. If that bar of justice exists—and our consciences bear witness to the fact that it does—then we need a true advocate.

Now let's think about what an advocate does for you. If you are accused of a crime and you go to court, what is your defense attorney to you? There is a sense in which, in court, your defense attorney *is* you. As the theologian Charles Hodge once said, in court you disappear into your advocate. If you stammer but your lawyer is eloquent, what do you look like in court? Eloquent. If you are ignorant but your lawyer is brilliant, what do you look like in court? Brilliant. In some cases, you may not be required to speak or even to appear personally in court. Your attorney appears in your place, as your substitute. So what do you look like in court? You look like whatever your advocate looks like. If your advocate wins, you win. If your advocate loses, you lose. In short, you're lost in your advocate—you are *in* your advocate.

Now we see the power of what John says to us in 1 John 2:1. He says that if you are guilty before the bar of justice and even before your own conscience, what do you need? A good example? A supportive helper? Do you need somebody who can show you how to pick yourself up and try harder? Someone who comes alongside and says, "You can do it!" Someone who knows the law and can tell us how you've broken it? Yes, you need those, but they are not your primary need. You need not just a good lawyer but a perfect Advocate to appear for you before the Father.

But we must take the metaphor one step further. If we are accused in court, we don't just need an eloquent and intelligent advocate; we need one who has a *case* to make.

In the early days after becoming a Christian, I first heard of this idea that Jesus Christ somehow "intercedes" for me before the Father. I got this out of the book of Hebrews, where Jesus is depicted as our great high priest who stands before the Father for us, as priests in the Old Testament did for the people. When I first heard the idea of Jesus Christ representing me before the Father, it made me think of him going before the throne like this: "Good morning, Father, I represent Tim Keller. And my client, I admit it, is having a very bad week. He's broken three or four promises he made to you. He has broken several of your laws that he knows and acknowledges. He has sinned a lot this week. He deserves to be punished— but cut him a break, please, Father? For my sake? I really ask that you give him another chance." That's how I imagined him speaking. And I also imagined the Father saying in reply, "Well, all right. Okay. For you, one more chance."

Now, the trouble with that imaginary scenario is that Jesus does not have a case; he is simply pleading for another chance. And I remember thinking, "I wonder how long even Jesus can keep that sort of thing up?" I wondered when the Father would finally say, "That does it! I've had it!" But my imagination was ill-informed. It is not sufficient for a lawyer to just resort to tugging on the heartstrings of the jury or the judge, or to try to delay the verdict, or to appeal to technicalities. The lawyer doesn't need spin or emotional manipulation—but a real case. And that is just what Jesus has.

What is his case? John goes on to tell us in 1 John 2:2. First, he says, "He is the atoning sacrifice for our sins." When Jesus goes before the Father, he is not actually asking for mercy for us. Of course it was infinitely merciful of God to send Christ to die for us, but that mercy has now been granted, so Jesus does not need to beg for it. 1 John 1:9 says that "if we confess our sins, he is faithful and *just* to forgive us our sins." Notice it does not say that if Christians confess their sins God forgives because he mercifully gives them another chance. No, it says he forgives because he is faithful and just. To not forgive us would be unjust. How could that be?

The best way for you to get an acquittal for your legal client is not to hope you can get some sympathy from the court. The best way is to show that your client *must* be acquitted under the law. You want to be able to say with integrity and conviction, "This is the law, and the law demands my client's acquittal." You want to make a case that is not based on how the court feels at the time but is open and shut according to the law. And Jesus has one! Jesus Christ can say, in effect, "Father, my people have sinned, and the law demands that the wages of sin be death. But I have paid for those sins. See, here is my blood, the token of my death! On the cross I have paid the penalty for these sins completely. Now, if anyone were to exact two payments for the same sin, it would be unjust. And so—I am not asking for mercy for them; I'm asking for justice."

That, if Jesus' claims are true, is an infallible case. This is why John could say that when Christians confess their sins they are forgiven because the justice of God now demands it! Every other philosophy and every other religion in the world essentially looks at life like the scales of justice. Remember the lady wearing the blindfold and holding the scales? In this metaphor, you're on one side of the scale. And on the other side is the law of God. It says, "Put God first. Love everyone. Obey the Golden Rule." And the law of God is stacked against you, dragging down the scale. You then have to spend the rest of your life desperately piling good works and merit and a disciplined life on your side of the scale to offset the weight of the law of God. In other words, the law of God is set up against you, and you had better live a good life or else it's going to outweigh you and be your doom. The law of God is constantly pointing toward your condemnation, and you must offset or neutralize it.

But guess what. If Jesus is your Advocate, the law of God is now completely *for* you. It's on your side of the scale. When you put your faith in Jesus, when you say from the heart, "Father, accept me because of what Jesus did," then Jesus' work on the cross is transferred to your account. Now the law of God demands your acquittal. That is why when John calls Jesus our Advocate, he also calls him "the Righteous One." This phrase suggests that when God looks at you, if you are a Christian, he sees you "in Christ." In yourself, alone on your side of the scale, you are a sinner; but in him you are perfect, just, beautiful, righteous. You're lost in your Advocate.

Paul wrote in 2 Corinthians 5:21, "God made him who had no sin to be sin for us, so that in him we might become the righteousness of God." That means that just as Jesus was not personally sinful but was treated as sinful and punished on the cross, now we who believe in him, while not personally righteous and perfect, are treated as righteous, beautiful, and perfect by the Father, for Jesus' sake.

So what is the job of the first Advocate? It is to say before the Father, "Look at what I've done. And now, accept them in me." Then what is the job of the other Advocate, whom Jesus promises to send them—the Holy Spirit? Remember that we will never understand the work of the second Advocate until we understand the work of the first. Many people say that the Holy Spirit gives us power, and that's true, but how does he do that? Does he merely zap us with higher energy levels? No—by calling him the *other* Advocate, Jesus has given us the great clue to understanding how the empowering of the Holy Spirit works.

The first Advocate is speaking to God for you, but the second Advocate is speaking to *you* for you. Throughout the Farewell Discourse, Jesus keeps saying that the job of the Spirit is to take all the things Jesus has done on our behalf—all the things that the apostles had still not yet grasped—and to "teach you" and "remind you" and enable the apostles to finally understand all that Jesus had taught them about his saving work (John 14:26). Theologian J. I. Packer has taught that the Holy Spirit's ministry is much like that of a floodlight. If you walk by a building at night and it's floodlit, you say, "Look at that beautiful building." You may not even see where the light is coming from. The floodlight's job is not to show you itself but to show you the beauty of the building, to throw all of its features into relief.

In the upper room the night before the cross, the apostles still don't have the slightest idea of how much he loves them, what it will cost him to love them, or what his love will accomplish for them. All of that is opaque to them. Therefore, though they have actually lived with him for three years, they haven't encountered the real Jesus. They still don't know him. But the Holy Spirit will come. And he will not merely hold their hand or give them energy—he will teach them deep, life-changing truth. He will finally help them see the depth of their sin (John 16:9). And he will finally show them what Jesus did for them.

I love the fact that the Holy Spirit is not merely an instructor, but an Advocate. Though he is "the Spirit of truth," he does not merely teach and inform us; he calls us to live according to what he is telling us. He convicts us and challenges us (John 16:8–11). He says in effect, "You are a sinner—are you living with the humility and dependence on God that results from that fact? Yet you are also righteous in Christ—adopted and accepted into the family. Are you living with the boldness and freedom that should accord with that fact? Are you as free from the need for worldly power and approval and comfort as you should be?" He argues with us, he exhorts, beseeches, and entreats us (all good translations of *parakaleo*), to live lives in accordance with the accomplishments and realities of Christ's love. And this is why Jesus says that through the Holy Spirit he will finally "show" himself to his friends (John 14:21). They will finally see him and know his loving presence.

Do you see the implication? The apostles did not—*could not*—truly know Jesus until he went away bodily and returned through the Holy Spirit. This is so encouraging for Christians to see. For instance, it's natural for us to believe that it would have been better to have lived during the time of Christ and to have actually met him and heard him with our ears and seen him with our eyes. You might believe that you could know him better that way than you do now—but you would be wrong. Before he died, the Holy Spirit had not been released into the world in this powerful way, and you can only know Jesus fully through the Spirit's influence, as he shows you in the shadow of the cross how high and long and wide and deep his love is for us. In other words, right here and now, through the Holy Spirit, you can see Christ and know his presence and his love better than the apostles could in that moment in the upper room.

If you're a Christian, it's likely that you're not living as if this is true. You probably don't see the magnitude of what is being offered to you in the Holy Spirit. Imagine you're a billionaire, and you have three ten-dollar bills in your wallet. You get out of a cab, and you hand the driver one of the bills for an eight-dollar fare. Later in the day you look in and find out there's only one ten-dollar bill there, and you say, "Either I dropped a ten-dollar bill somewhere, or I gave the taxi driver two bills." What are you going to do? Are you going to get all upset? Are you going to disrupt the rest of your day? Are you going to the police and demand they search the city for the cabdriver? No, you are going to shrug. You're a billionaire. You lost ten dollars. So what? You are too rich to be concerned about that kind of loss.

This week, somebody criticized you. Something you bought or invested in turned out to be less valuable than you thought. Something you wanted to happen didn't go the way you wanted it to. Someone you counted on let you down. These are real losses—of your reputation, of your material wealth, of your hopes. But what are you going to do, if you're a Christian? Will this setback disrupt your contentment with life? Will you shake your fist at God? Toss and turn at night? If so, I submit that it's because you don't know how truly rich you are. You are not listening to the second Advocate about your first Advocate. You are not living in joy. You are forgetting that the only eyes in the universe that matter see you not as the "phony little fake" you have sometimes been, but as a person of captivating beauty. If you're that upset about your status with other people, if you're constantly lashing out at people for hurting your feelings, you might call it a lack of self-control or a lack of self-esteem, and it is. But more fundamentally, you have totally lost touch with your identity. As a Christian, you're a spiritual billionaire and you're wringing your hands over ten dollars. It's the job of the second Advocate to argue with you in the court of your heart, to make the case about who you are in Christ, to show you that you're rich. And it's your job to listen.

How can you listen better? That's a big subject, but if you are a believer, then the Holy Spirit will do his work as you use the "means of grace"—reading and studying the Word by yourself and in community, prayer, worship, and the sacraments of baptism and the Lord's Supper. If you don't use the means of grace, you are not giving the other Advocate scope to do his work. Or if you attend these things in a thoughtless, perfunctory way, you will be technically present but closing your ears to his instruction, comfort, counsel, and advocacy.

If you don't experience the work of the second Advocate, your loss cannot be measured. Jesus says, "Peace I leave with you; my peace I give you. I do not give to you as the world gives." Without the work of the Spirit you can't know Jesus or know his peace. How is the world's peace different from Jesus' peace? First, today we are often told we can get peace by avoiding thinking too much about the big questions of life. I had a friend some years ago who was a medical student. He told me that in medical school he had learned how fragile the human body was, how many things could go wrong so easily, and how many millions of viruses and microbes were out there, ready to attack at any time. He said that it unnerved him. I asked him how he was dealing with his fear and he said that he had forced himself not to think about it. By and large that's how the world's "peace" works. Life is nasty, brutish, and short—and then you die. Just don't think about it. But Christ's peace works in the opposite way, not through less thinking, but through more. Not by ignoring reality, but by paying attention to it. The Holy Spirit tells you the Father loves you; your eternal bliss is guaranteed. In other words, Christ gives us true things to think about that overcome the darkness of this life, while the world can only say, "Just hum loudly and look away."

Also, though Christian peace can be consistent, the world's peace is intermittent, because it is based on circumstances. People like you, the money is coming in, your job is fine, you've just made a deal, you're in a beautiful setting, and you feel peaceful. But when the stock market's down and you've had a failure, you're down. You're agitated. Why? Because your peace depends on your circumstances.

I once heard the story of an eighteenth-century Welsh preacher who, when he was just a teenager, was standing with his family around the deathbed of one of his aunts. His aunt had been a strong Christian, but now she was slipping away. Everyone thought she was unconscious and some said out loud, "It's a shame; she's had such a hard life. She's seen two husbands die, and she's often been sick, and on top of it all she has died poor." Suddenly she opened her eyes, looked around, and said, "Who calls me poor? I am rich, rich! And I will soon stand before Him bold as a lion." And then she died.

Understandably, that had quite an effect on the young man. This woman had the peace that Jesus spoke of because she had listened to the Advocate. She was saying, "I've got the only husband who can't die. I've got the only wealth that can never go away. And my Savior dealt long ago with sin—the only disease that can really and truly kill me. How can you call me poor?" The second Advocate had told her about the first Advocate, so she could say in the face of great loss, as the hymn writer did, "It is well, it is well with my soul."[24]

And so it can be with yours. The Spirit, the second Advocate, may even be speaking to you right now. Let him tell you, "Yes. Jesus is your Advocate. Isn't he beautiful? Put your faith in him." If you put your faith in the work of Jesus Christ you can stand even before that seat of judgment bold as a lion. God sees you spotless, without blemish, so that you can sing,

> Well may the Accuser roar
> Of sins that I have done.
> I know them all and thousands more.
> Jehovah knoweth none.

So that is what Jesus was telling his disciples in the upper room. This was his lifeline to those who had failed him in life and would change the world after his death. "Believe in me and receive the Spirit when I am gone. Listen to him about my infallible case and he will give you an infallible peace." Whether or not you yet consider yourself a spiritual descendant of those disciples, these words are meant for you as well.

EIGHT

THE OBEDIENT MASTER

Often Jesus' time in the garden of Gethsemane before his death is seen as an interesting and convicting example of the weakness of his disciples, who are even at that near-final hour clueless about what Jesus is about to undergo. But Jesus' experience in that dark place was not really an interlude between events of higher and more significant dramatic action. Something happened there that begs for a deeper explanation. There is perhaps nowhere else in the Bible where we get a more penetrating look at Jesus' own inner life, motivation, and experience. This scene throws as much light on why and how he died, and how we should respond to it, as any other part of the Gospel accounts—including the crucifixion narratives.

To get the full picture of what happened, we should look at the accounts of Matthew, Mark, and Luke. Here is the beginning of the scene, according to Matthew:

Then Jesus went with his disciples to a place called Gethsemane, and he said to them, "Sit here while I go over there and pray." He took Peter and the two sons of Zebedee along with him, and he began to be sorrowful and troubled. Then he said to them, "My soul is overwhelmed with sorrow to the point of death. Stay here and keep watch with me." (Matthew 26:36–38)

First I want to examine the magnitude of the pain Christ experienced here. Matthew, Mark, and Luke each find a way to tell us that Jesus' grief and sorrow were enormous, well beyond even what we would expect at such a moment. Matthew records Jesus' words "My soul is overwhelmed with sorrow to the point of death." He was experiencing an internal and mental agony so unbearable that he felt like the pain alone could kill him right then and there.

Now, Jesus is called "a Man of Sorrows." Throughout his life we see him weeping and sighing much more than we see him exulting. But this burden is something far greater. Matthew indicates that as Jesus was walking away from the larger group of disciples with Peter, James, and John toward the garden for prayer, "he *began* [emphasis mine] to be sorrowful and troubled" (Matthew 26:37). This change happens as he is en route—it almost seems to descend upon him in real time. Not only was this mental agony so enormous that he thought he was going to die, but according to Mark he was astounded by it. Mark uses the Greek word *ekthambeisthai*, which means to be moved to an "intense emotional state because of something causing great surprise or perplexity."[25] Some English translations mute the meaning of this term and just translate it as "deeply distressed" (as in the New International Version). I wonder if that is because we have a feeling that if Jesus really is who he says he is—the infinitely preexistent Son of God come to earth—he couldn't be thunderstruck by anything. How could the Second Person of the Trinity, who even in his human form seems to anticipate every eventuality, be shocked? But he is. He's reeling, dumbfounded, astonished. As he is on his way to pray, a darkness and horror comes down on him beyond anything he could have anticipated, and the pain of it makes him feel he is disintegrating on the spot.

Consider that all the Gospel writers knew by the time they wrote their accounts that many of Jesus' own followers were able to face death with remarkable serenity. Luke records that when the Christian leader Stephen faced his executioners, his radiant "face was like the face of an angel" (Acts 6:15), and as they stoned him to death he gently prayed for their forgiveness (Acts 7:60). Early Christian writers such as Ignatius of Antioch and Polycarp pointed to the poise with which Christians faced torture and death. One historian writes that this was one of the ways that Christian thinkers attempted to recommend their faith to the pagan population. They argued that Christians suffered and died better than pagans.[26] Christians went to the lions singing hymns; they went into the flames with their hands raised in prayer.

But Jesus Christ is facing death in a way that his followers did not. His face is not as radiant as the face of an angel. He is not calm or poised or at peace. And certainly this must have really happened. If Matthew, Mark, and Luke were making up or even just embellishing the life of the founder of their faith, would they depict him struggling more desperately before his imminent death than most of his followers?

What is the reason, then, for the magnitude of Jesus' agony and horror before his death? The answer is, this was a different death than anybody else ever faced before or since.

Here is the next part of Matthew's account:

> Going a little farther, he fell with his face to the ground and prayed, "My Father, if it is possible, may this cup be taken from me. Yet not as I will, but as you will."
>
> Then he returned to his disciples and found them sleeping. "Couldn't you men keep watch with me for one hour?" he asked Peter. "Watch and pray so that you will not fall into temptation. The spirit is willing, but the flesh is weak."
>
> He went away a second time and prayed, "My

Father, if it is not possible for this cup to be taken
away unless I drink it, may your will be done."

When he came back, he again found them sleeping, because their eyes were heavy. So he left them
and went away once more and prayed the third
time, saying the same thing. (Matthew 26:39–44)

Matthew, Mark, and Luke all mention "the cup" as the
heart of Jesus' prayer that night. The cup, in ancient times, was
like the electric chair. Remember how Socrates was
executed—he drank a cup of poison. "The cup" did not represent just any kind of death in general but rather a judicial
death in particular. The apostles' use of the term means that
Jesus knows he is going to be executed. But it means even
more than that.

In the Bible "the cup" further refers to God's own judicial
wrath on injustice and evildoing. Ezekiel 23 says, "You will
drink . . . the cup of ruin and desolation . . . and you will tear
your breasts," and Isaiah 51 speaks of those who drink "the cup
of his wrath . . . the bowl of staggering." The reason that Jesus
Christ did not die as gracefully as later Christian martyrs is because none of them were facing the cup. When Jesus himself
speaks of the cup, it shows he knows that he is facing not just
physical torture and death; he is about to experience the full divine wrath on the evil and sin of all humanity. The judicial wrath
of God is about to come down upon him rather than upon us.

And while this outpouring of wrath struck with full force on the cross the next day—where Jesus cried out, "My God, my God, why have you forsaken me?"—I agree with the commentators who believe that he was beginning to get his first experiential foretaste of it here in the garden. What would that judicial wrath feel like? It is the torture of divine absence.

2 Thessalonians 1:8 reads: "He will punish those who do not know God and do not obey the gospel of our Lord Jesus." The judgment of God in the Bible is unbelievably fair. It is an utterly natural consequence. The essence of sin is "I do not want to have God in my life." And the essence of God's judicial wrath is to give us what we have asked for. There truly is nothing fairer than that—and nothing more terrible. According to the Bible we are all built for God, made to enjoy his presence and a relationship with him. Here on earth, even those of us who disbelieve and flee from God are not completely cut off from him. Paul says that in God "we live and move and have our being" (Acts 17:28). He was speaking to Greek philosophers at the time, people who didn't believe in God. He meant that even though we may not acknowledge the God of the Bible, he is still upholding our lives in ways we cannot see. And what would happen if God were to truly remove his gracious, sustaining power from our lives? It would be a kind of spiritual agony and disintegration that would go on forever, since our souls are built for his love and presence. It would be eternal torment and perfectly just. As C. S. Lewis says in *The Great*

Divorce, if in this life you never say to God, "Thy will be done," then eventually God will say to you for the afterlife, "All right, then *thy* will be done." If you want freedom from God, you will quite justly get what you hope for. And it will be torment.

Now think back to Jesus Christ in the garden. As a human being on earth, God sustained his sentient human existence, and Jesus had access to the joy of God's presence in regular prayer and communion with the Father. Yet unlike any other human being, he would have shared the perfect intensity of the love of God. He would have known the infinite bliss of full fellowship with the Father. But as he was walking into the garden, he would have started to pray, and suddenly—for the first time in all of eternity—he would find the lines of communication severed. This is what Bill Lane, who has written a commentary on Mark, says about the garden (emphasis mine):

> That dreadful sorrow and anxiety then, out of which the prayer for the passing of the cups brings, is not an expression of fear before a dark destiny, nor a shrinking from the prospect of physical suffering and death. It is rather *the horror of one who lives wholly for the Father at the prospect of the alienation from God which is entailed in the judgment upon sin which Jesus assumes. . . .* Jesus came to be with the Father . . . before his betrayal, but hell rather than heaven opened before him, and he staggered.[27]

Remember what Ezekiel and Isaiah said. The cup of God's wrath is like a poison that makes the body stagger and burn with inner pain. That is what is beginning to happen to Jesus. He begins to pray and he suddenly sees into the abyss. No Father, no presence, no communion; Hell rather than Heaven opens to his gaze. And the only way to conceive of the infinite magnitude of his sufferings is to realize that he is the Son of God. If I were to lose the love of a friend, that would be painful. If I were to lose the love of my children or my wife, that would be infinitely more painful. The longer, deeper, and more intimate the love relationship, the more searing the pain when it is severed. But the Son's perfect love relationship with the Father is as far beyond my love relationship with my wife as an ocean is beyond a dewdrop. And this is what he was losing.

Yet Jesus' predicament was worse than even that, for he began to experience not merely the absence of love but the presence of wrath. And just as divine love is immeasurably beyond human love, so the experience of divine wrath must be beyond human anger. God is omnipotent—infinitely powerful. How can we imagine what it would be like for a mountain of divine wrath to come down on us? How much does omnipotence weigh?

Luke's Gospel says that Jesus was literally "in agony" (in Greek, *agonia*—translated in the NIV as "anguish") and adds that, as he prayed, his profuse sweat was "like drops of blood." It is possible this means there was blood in his sweat—since people in great shock can burst capillaries near the surface of their skin, causing blood to seep out with their perspiration. Or it may mean that the rivers of sweat were like the blood that would soon be pouring out and running down his body. Either way, he is in extremity. He is beginning to experience the incredible agony of being cut off from the Father—such that he falls to the ground and begs, "Don't let this happen."

So why the magnitude of the agony? Because Jesus Christ was not simply dying as any other person would die. He was losing his perfect communion with the Father on our account. And as our substitute, he was receiving the judicial wrath of God. Jonathan Edwards summarized it like this: "The conflict in Christ's soul, in this view of his last sufferings, was dreadful, beyond all expression or conception."

I also want to look at the timing of Jesus' agony. With the help of theologians like William Lane and Jonathan Edwards, I've argued that Jesus was getting a foretaste of the divine wrath here in the garden. But why is it particularly important that he experiences that foretaste so greatly now, before the moment of the crucifixion? The answer gets at a part of Christian doctrine that is often overlooked or misunderstood but is deeply consoling.

Theologians over the years have made a distinction between the passive and active aspects of Christ's work. It is taught that in his passive obedience, Jesus took the penalty we deserved; he died the death we should have died. But in his active obedience, he lived the life we should have lived.[28] This may sound esoteric, but it is actually quite practical.

When Jesus went to the cross, he took upon himself the punishment for sins that we deserve and that he didn't. That is what has historically been called his "passive" work: He received the penalty for our disobedience to God's law. As a result, we who believe in Jesus are free from any condemnation for those sins. But if this was all he had done for us, we might be grateful that we will not be punished for things we have done in the past. We might be supremely relieved that God won't be angry with us anymore. But we still wouldn't have evidence that he actually loves us, for just because a father is not punishing his son doesn't mean he's delighted with him. And so if you believed only in Jesus' passive work, you might still feel under a great deal of pressure and fear that you were not truly "right with God" and could still lose God's favor if you slipped up. You could know you were pardoned, but you certainly could not be assured that you were loved.

But passively absorbing punishment is not all Jesus did for us. During his entire life, and preeminently here at his death, he also fulfilled the positive demands of the law of God as well, which has been called his "active" work. Jesus not only died the death we should have died in order to take the law's curse for us, he also lived the great life of love and fidelity we should have lived in order to earn God's blessing for us. No one ever loved God with his entire soul, mind, and strength—

no one ever loved his neighbor with perfect, full, sacrificial love—except Jesus. What does a life like that deserve? It deserves God's highest blessing, praise, and honor. It deserves God's full love and delight. And because Jesus not only fulfilled the law of God passively but actively—in our place, as our substitute—it means not only that he got the penalty we deserved, we get the reward from God that he deserved. It's an astonishingly *thorough* salvation, with grace piled on top of grace.

What does this have to do with Jesus' struggles in the garden of Gethsemane? Wasn't that just the beginning of Jesus' passive obedience—dying for us? No; it was more than that.

It is one thing to know something cognitively in the abstract and quite another thing to know it with one's whole being. We may know in our minds that the experience in the dentist's chair will hurt, but we make the appointment and we jump into the chair with a nervous joke. But as soon as the drilling begins we say to ourselves, "If I had known it was going to be like this, I would never have come. It's not worth it." Now what if somehow while you were still at home deciding to schedule the appointment you could have, for a minute or two, a foretaste of what the actual pain would be like? If that were possible, most of the world's dentists would be out of business.

Up until now, Jesus certainly *knew* what was to come. He had been constantly telling his disciples he had come to suffer and die. We saw earlier that the shadow of this night loomed before him at the wedding in Cana; and that he healed Lazarus knowing that it would set in motion the events that would lead to the cross. But his astonishment as he entered the garden reveals that only now is he experientially grasping what he is about to endure. The next day out in public he will be nailed to the cross, and at that point there will be no escaping his fate. But here in the dark, with the disciples asleep, when Jesus could very easily slip away, the Father lets him know what he is in for. As Jonathan Edwards says in his "Christ's Agony" sermon, "It was the first time that Christ had a full view of the difficulty of this command; which appeared so great as to cause that bloody sweat." And so, when he goes to the cross for us after this experience in the garden, he goes with vivid firsthand knowledge of what will happen. And that makes Jesus' action the greatest act of love to the Father—and to his fellow human beings—in the history of the world. No one ever faced suffering like this in order to love, and so no one ever loved like this. Edwards continues:

> The agony of Jesus Christ was caused by a vivid, bright, full, immediate view of the wrath of God. God the Father, as it were, set the cup down before him, which was vastly more terrible than Nebuchadnezzar's furnace. He now had a near view of the furnace into which he was about to be cast. He stood

and viewed the raging flames and the glowings of its heat that he might know where he was going and what he was about to suffer. He felt what Ezekiel said, "You shall drink the cup of ruin and desolation and tear your breasts." He felt what Isaiah said, that you will "drink the cup of his wrath . . . the bowl of staggering." Christ was going to be cast into a dreadful furnace of wrath and it was not proper that he should plunge himself into it blindfold as not knowing how dreadful the furnace was. Therefore God brought him and set him at the mouth of the furnace that he might look in and stand and view its fierce and raging flames and might see where he was going and might voluntarily enter into it and bear it for us, knowing what it was. If Jesus Christ did not full know before he took it, and drunk it, it would not properly have been his own act as a human being. But when he took that cup knowing what he did, so was his love to us infinitely more wonderful and his obedience to God infinitely more perfect.

God set the cup in front of Jesus, as it were, and let him smell it and taste it when it was still possible for Jesus to pull away and protect himself. In effect, the Father was saying, "Here's the cup that you are about to drink. Here is the furnace into which you are about to be cast. See these friends of yours sleeping over there? If they are to be saved, there is no other way. Either they perish, or you perish. See how terrible the heat is, see what pain and anguish you must endure. Is your love for them and for me so great that you will go on and take it?"

And Edwards imagines that Jesus could have looked at his disciples, who could not even stay awake to support him in the hour of his greatest need, and said with complete justice and warrant:

> Why should I, who have been living from all eternity in the enjoyment of the Father's love, go to cast myself into such a furnace for them that never can requite me for it? Why should I yield myself to be thus crushed by the weight of divine wrath, for them who have no love to me, and are my enemies? They do not deserve any union with me, and never did, and never will do any thing to recommend themselves to me.

He *could* rightly have said this—but he didn't. That was not the language of his heart. Instead he said to God, "Thy will be done." Edwards concludes: "His sorrows abounded, but his love did much more abound. Christ's soul was overwhelmed with a deluge of grief, but this was from a deluge of love to sinners in his heart sufficient to overflow the world, and overwhelm the highest mountains of its sins. Those great drops of blood that fell down to the ground were a manifestation of an ocean of love in Christ's heart."

As we have been saying, it is not enough to say this was only the greatest act of love in history; it was also the most astounding, perfect act of obedience to God. At the beginning of history there was also a garden and a command. God put Adam and Eve in that garden, and they were told not to eat of the Tree. The direction was: "Obey me about the Tree, and you will live"—obey me and I'll bless you. But they disobeyed. Now there is another garden, and a Second Adam,[29] and another command. Jesus Christ has been sent by the Father to go to the cross, which is also a tree.[30]

Now the command of God to Adam was the prototype for all his commands to everyone. God always says, in one way or another, "Obey me and I will bless you; I will be with you." But here is the exception. Only once has he said to a human being what he says to Jesus. To the first Adam he said, "Obey me about the Tree and I will bless you"—and Adam didn't do it. But to the second Adam he says, "Obey me about the Tree and I will crush you"—and Jesus does. Jesus is the first and last person in history to be told that obedience would bring a curse. The Father is saying, essentially, "If you obey me, if you are faithful to me, I will forsake you, cast you off and send your soul into hell." And yet Jesus obeyed. Even as he was dying, abandoned by his Father, he called him "My God"—words that in the Bible were covenant language, conveying intimacy.

Even though he was being forsaken, Jesus was still obeying. The poet George Herbert, again referring to the cross as a tree, puts beautifully how the disobedience of the first Adam was put right only through the far more difficult and greater obedience of the second. Herbert imagines Jesus speaking from the cross, saying:

> O all ye who passe by, behold and see;
> Man stole the fruit, but I must climb the tree;
> The tree of life to all, but onely me:
> Was ever grief like mine?

And now return to that seemingly esoteric teaching about the passive and active obedience of Christ. If Jesus had died only the death I should have died, then if I wanted to be sure that the Father not only pardoned me but loved me deeply and fully, I would rightly feel it was up to me to live a morally heroic life. My sins would be forgiven, but God's positive regard of me otherwise would be completely dependent on how well I was living.

But Jesus did not just die the death we should have died; he lived the life we should have lived. As one Scottish minister, Robert Murray M'Cheyne, used to say, he is not just a dying savior, he is a doing savior. When we believe in him, we do not just get the benefits of his death. It is not just that our sins are forgiven, but we also get the benefits of his obedience. That means his righteousness is credited to us (theologians use the financial term *imputed*), as well as his sacrifice. In 2 Corinthians 5:21, it says: "God made him who had no sin to be sin for us, so that we might become the righteousness of God in him." When we believe in Jesus Christ, we are seen as righteous. We are seen as obeying. We are seen in our Advocate. We are seen to be doing as well as Jesus did, not just dying as well as Jesus died.

And look at the beauty, the power of what Jesus did! What kind of honor does this kind of valor, this level of love and sacrifice deserve? That's the honor that comes to you when you believe in Christ. On a TV detective show some years ago I saw a story of a man in his eighties, an ex-Marine, sadly broken down and accused of a crime. Two big, strapping military police and a snarling Navy lawyer come to arrest him. They are speaking brusquely and barking orders when suddenly one of the old man's friends reaches over and pulls away his tie. There is revealed the Congressional Medal of Honor, which he had won decades before at Iwo Jima. At the sight of that medal the lawyer and the MPs snap suddenly to attention. They are not saluting him personally, of course. In himself he might be a criminal and in many other ways is certainly a failure. But for the sake of the medal—which represented not only his sacrificial deeds but the valor of hundreds of others in military service over the centuries—he was treated with honor. That's just a partial hint of what happens to us in light of Christ's active obedience. We are not like prisoners who are freed and given bus fare downtown from the prison. No, we are like prisoners who are freed and then draped with the Medal of Honor, with all the rights and benefits that would come with it. We are not just given pardon and freedom but love and delight. That's the active obedience of Jesus at work. And though he has been obeying God by living a perfect life throughout, his active obedience faces a monumental challenge here in the garden. That's why it's so important that we see the beauty of his response to that challenge, before he has passed the point of no return.

Now, what difference does all this make for us? How does it help us, to see Jesus suffer something we will never experience?

First, Jesus in the garden is an unparalleled model of integrity. In the dark, with nobody looking, knowing that he is called to do the hardest thing anyone has ever done, Jesus still does the right thing. He does the same thing in the dark and in private that the next day he will do in full view. Let me ask you—are you the same person in the dark as you are in the light? Are you the same in private as you are in public? Or are you living a double life?

Second, this is not only a great model for integrity, it is a great model for prayer. The most astounding thing about Jesus is that he is, at the same moment, both brutally honest about his feelings and desires and yet absolutely submitted to the will of God. He is honest—he doesn't put on a pious front. Three times the Son of God tells the Father he'd prefer to avoid the plan of salvation. There is no cover-up. And yet he says, without hesitating, "Not my will, but thy will be done." The basic purpose of prayer is not to bend God's will to mine but to mold my will into his. Jesus is so God-centered and yet so human and honest at once. Let this be your guide for prayer. You must neither repress your feelings nor be ruled by them. Most people do one or the other, but not both.

Third, in the garden we have a tremendous example of patience with people. In Matthew's account he comes back to his disciples at one point and says, "Couldn't you men keep watch with me for one hour?" (Matthew 26:40). Here is a man under the most crushing weight asking his friends for a little support and finding that they have gone to sleep on him. He has been completely let down, but what does he say? Matthew records Jesus' words: "The spirit is willing, but the flesh is weak" (Matthew 26:41). Isn't that remarkable? He is giving them some credit. He says, "You let me down, but I know you mean well." In the depths of his agony he can still find something affirming to say to his friends. There are about twenty things wrong with the disciples' performance that night, but he finds the one or two things that are right and points them out. "Having loved his own who were in the world, he loved them to the end" (John 13:1).

So Jesus is a great model of how to live, pray, and relate to people. But remember that if Jesus is *only* a model for us, then he is no encouragement—for he is too good. No one could live up to his standard. Jesus came not just to be a model but a savior. He changes us on the inside so that we can be slowly but surely made over into his image. He does not just tell us how to live; he gives us the power to live that way. The paradox is that only if we see him as a substitute rather than a model can we actually have the ability to live according to his model.

How? Look at him here in the garden, doing all this not just as an example but as a substitute, in your place. Knowing that makes his suffering personal to you. It can give you a new ability to face your own trials, to rid yourself of crippling self-pity and lack of resolve. Think of God, swirling the cup right under Jesus' nose, saying, "Are you really going to do that for these people?" And Jesus says, "Yes." Whenever you are feeling sorry for yourself—"Oh my, what a cup I am drinking"—you can say to yourself, "Oh, but it is *nothing* like his cup! What I am going through is nothing compared to what he did." And so you can pray something like this: "Lord, you were patient in your infinite suffering for me. I can certainly be patient in this much smaller suffering for you."

The teaching of Christ's active obedience also transforms your self-regard and makes a new ballast and poise available to you. Jesus not only pardoned you; he also pinned his "Medal of Honor" on you. When you believe in him you are not just forgiven but beautiful to God, righteous in Him. Now, how do you deal with criticism or failure? We should not look at who we are in ourselves but at who we are in him. Oftentimes after we screw up, we realize upon reflection that we were trying to save face, scrambling for reputation or approval. In other words, we try to prove ourselves, make ourselves beautiful, significant, and righteous—though we wouldn't use those terms. We are trying to make ourselves feel important and decent, instead of letting Jesus carry the burden of significance. If we really understood how God regards us in Christ, we could take disapproval and failure in stride.

But there is another thing that this passage gives us. I know people who have said: "I would follow Christ, but I do not think I can keep it up. I do not trust myself. I think he'd get tired of my failures." Please look at him in the garden. Look what his love for you has already enabled him to endure for you. If he had turned away from suffering and the cross, we would have been lost, but he didn't do that. Hell came down on him, and he would not let go of us. His love for us has already taken everything that the universe could throw at it and it held fast—and you think that you are somehow going to upset him? Is Jesus going to look at you and say, "Well, that does it! Infinite existential torment was one thing, but I can only take so much!"?

If the cup did not make him give up on us, nothing will. So Paul can essentially say, "Nothing can separate us from the love of Christ" (Romans 8:38–39). The Lord says, "I will never leave you; never will I forsake you" (Hebrews 13:5).

This is the love you have been looking for all of your life. This is the only love that can't let you down. This is bomb-proof love. Not friend-love, not personal acclaim, not married love, and not even romantic love—it is this love that you are after, underneath all your pursuit of those others. And if this love of active obedience is an active reality in your life, you will be a person of integrity; you will be a person of prayer; you will be kind to people who mistreat you. If you have this love, you will be a little more like him. Look at him dying in the dark for you. Let it melt you into his likeness.

NINE

THE RIGHT HAND OF THE FATHER

And so we come to the very last act of Jesus Christ on earth—his ascension to the right hand of the Father in heaven—and it may be the most puzzling of all these milestone events. First, of course, the ascension was puzzling to the disciples who witnessed it. It was perhaps the most visually unexpected of all the miracles they had seen firsthand. In Acts 1:9–11, we read, "After he [spoke], he was taken up before their very eyes, and a cloud hid him from their sight." As he went off into the sky the apostles stood staring at the heavens like deer gazing into headlights, not understanding what was going on. "They were looking intently up into the sky as he was going, when suddenly two men dressed in white stood beside them. 'Men of Galilee,' they said, 'why do you stand here looking into the sky? This same Jesus, who has been taken from you into heaven, will come back in the same way.' " We're not quite sure what the disciples were thinking as they stood staring at the clouds, but the two angels had to give them a gentle rebuke. "Snap out of it, men!" they were saying. "He left and he's coming back, but until then, there's work to do. So get a move on." Obviously, the apostles were puzzling over the meaning of the ascension from the moment it happened.

But the ascension is also puzzling for us. And for us, the question is not so much "What happened?" as "Why did it happen?" What difference does it really make for the state of our souls and for how we live? Certainly it makes sense that if there was a "coming down" in the incarnation there would be a "going back" in the ascension. But it is not immediately evident that the ascension makes a difference in our salvation or in the way we live.

Actually, it makes an enormous difference. The ascension, when understood, becomes an irreplaceable, important resource for living our lives in the world—and it's a resource no other religion or philosophy of life holds out to us. So let's explore what the apostles eventually learned about the ascension, which they recorded in various places in the New Testament. First we'll learn what the ascension is theologically and second what it means for us practically.

First, what is the ascension? It is not simply Jesus' return from the earth to heaven. It is a new enthronement for Jesus, ushering in a new relationship with us and with the whole world.

Let's start by thinking about what the ascension is *not*. The ascension is not simply Jesus leaving the surface of the earth.

It's not so much about him going into the heavens but rather into heaven. Do you remember that the premier of the Soviet Union said in 1961 that his pilot had gone up into the heavens and didn't see God there, so he must not exist? That reveals an understanding of the ascension to heaven as basically a change in altitude, such that Christ and the Father are somewhere in outer space. Now, the Bible does talk about "the heavens," as when Psalm 19 speaks of "the heavens [the sun, moon, and stars] telling of the glory of God" (New American Standard Bible). But Jesus didn't go into the heavens of the stars and planets. He went into Heaven with a capital *H*. And that is something far more profound than an orbit in outer space.

In fact, the word *ascend* is probably the right place to start. We know it means to go upward, like an aircraft, but we are usually quite careful when we apply the word to people. For example, we could say "he ascended the ladder," but we don't usually use so grand a word to describe such a thing. (Or if we did, it might be a bit tongue-in-cheek.) We would say instead that he climbed or went up the ladder. But we would certainly use the word to describe a coronation. When someone becomes a king or queen, there is a ceremony in which authority is officially transferred. The person literally walks up onto a podium and then goes up steps and sits on a throne, a higher chair. And we say, "She ascended to the throne." The word *ascended* gets across more than a change in elevation. She is not just physically higher than everyone else—she has a new relationship to others and has new powers and privileges to exercise authority. The steps and the higher chair are symbolic.

If you were to go to London you could find King Edward's Chair in Westminster Abbey. It has been the chair used in the coronations of the kings and queens of Britain for eight hundred years. And if you literally went up the steps and sat on that throne it wouldn't mean you'd actually have the royal job. (You would also be likely to get thrown out of Westminster Abbey, by the way.) The point is that ascension to a throne is not defined by a change in physical elevation (though that happens in the ceremony) but rather a change in legal status and relationship. Going up and sitting on the throne doesn't make you a monarch. And you can become the monarch of England without actually sitting in that old chair.

Now, if Jesus merely wanted to return to the Father, he could have just vanished. There were other times in which he vanished immediately out of sight, as with the disciples on the road to Emmaus. But instead, at the ascension Jesus literally rises up into the clouds and disappears into the distance of the heavens. Why did he do it that way? We can only speculate, but it may have been for the same reason that we have a coronation ceremony. The elevation in space symbolized the elevation in authority and relationship. Jesus was tracing out physically what was happening cosmically and spiritually.

And what was that? He was going, now as the unique God-man—fully human and fully divine—to take his place as the new king and head of the human race. Here is where Christian theology can push us out to the very edges of our thinking and imagination.

When the eternal Son of God "became flesh," he became fully human. Besides being vulnerable, subject to injury and death, he had the limitations of being confined to one place in time and space. Even after his resurrection Jesus could be touched and could eat normally. "A ghost does not have flesh and bones, as you see I have," he says in Luke 24:39, showing that he still has a human nature. Yet he has changed, too. He can appear through locked doors (John 20:19) and vanish (Luke 24:31). His human nature is still human but has undergone a transformation. And so here we have a picture of our own future. Jesus is, Paul writes, "the first fruits" of those who have died (1 Corinthians 15:20). Those who believe in him will eventually be resurrected like him. We will have human bodies, but they will be restored and enhanced to what we were before sin and evil crushed us. They will not be subject to decay or death. They will evidently also have many new powers and senses that we cannot now imagine.

But at the ascension another change takes place. As long as the man Jesus existed in the world of space and time, he could only be at one spot at one moment. If you wanted to hear him, relate to him, or experience him, you had to be at that place and that time. But at the ascension Jesus leaves the space-time continuum and passes into the presence of the Father. He is still human, still our second Adam (1 Corinthians 15:22) and still our Advocate—yet now he has been so glorified that everything he does has a cosmic scope. A hymn speaks of "rich wounds, yet visible above, in beauty glorified."[31] Louis Berkhof in his classic *Systematic Theology* says he "passed into the fullness of heavenly glory and was perfectly adapted for the life of heaven."[32] As a result, any time-space limitation to his work passes away. You no longer have to go to a single geographical location in order to receive his ministry. He's still doing all the things he did before, but now, after the ascension, he's doing them with access to anyone in any place and all at once. The ascension doesn't mean the loss of his intimacy, his leadership, and his advocacy; it means the magnification and infinite availability of all of these.

To put this in theological terms, Jesus is now (from heaven) "actively engaged in the continuation of his mediatorial work"[33] all across the globe. He is still our prophet, teaching and instructing us with his Word, but now he does it everywhere through the Holy Spirit. He is still our king, but now he guides and directs his entire church through the spiritual gifts he gives his people (Ephesians 4:4–16)—gifts of leadership, service, mercy, teaching, administration, and giving. And he is still our priest, counseling and supporting us, but now representing us before the very face of the Father.

In both Matthew 26:64 and Acts 2:33–36 the Bible says that in the ascension Jesus went "to the right hand of the

Father." In ancient times, whoever sat at the right hand of the throne was something like the king's prime minister, the one who executed his kingly authority and rule in actual laws and policies. And so this is saying that Jesus ascended to begin his reign. But this idea that the ascension is an enthronement requires some clarifications to be made. Jesus has always been king—he has always had authority over us because he is God. But now, at the ascension, as the risen God-man, he begins his job as heavenly head of the church, and now he rules over all other rulers and powers—indeed "over *everything* for the church" (Ephesians 1:21–22). He does this especially through the work of the Holy Spirit, work that Jesus laid out in detail to his disciples the night before he died (John 14–17). It also means he is ruling over and controlling all of history toward its final goal, in which the church, the new people of God, are finally and fully liberated, and, along with them, the whole world is renewed (Romans 8:18ff). And at that time there will be no more suffering, evil, or death, because Jesus' saving and restoring work will be complete. To put it simply, Jesus is directing a cosmic transition plan—one that will bring about new heavens and a new earth (Isaiah 65:17–25). As ascended Lord he is spreading the gospel and building up his church by working in the hearts of people while he guides all the events of history toward a glorious end.

So that is what the ascension is. But what does this mean for us practically? How does it affect how we live our daily lives? It means more than we can recount and explore here. But let's consider three important things.

First, the ascended Christ is a Jesus available for loving communication and fellowship. As we saw in chapter 5, when Mary Magdalene found the risen Christ near the empty tomb, she grabbed hold of him. Let's look at this incident again.

When she took hold of him, Jesus said to her, "Do not hold on to me, for I have not yet ascended to the Father" (John 20:17). What does that mean? Some people assume that Jesus is saying, "You must not touch me," as if he was sacred. The trouble with that theory is that later in the very same chapter he invites Thomas to touch him. So what does Jesus mean? The verb he uses when he says "don't hold on to me" is a word that means to squeeze tight. Mary had grabbed hold of him with all her might. It is likely that she was thinking that she had lost her cherished relationship with her teacher when he died and, now that he was alive, she would never allow it to be lost again.

But there she was mistaken. When Jesus said, "Don't hold on to me. . . . I am returning to my Father," he was indicating that after he ascended she'd have access to an even stronger love relationship. Why? Because then he would literally never leave her, and he would be not just in her arms sometimes but in her heart always. Here's the gist of what I think he was saying: "Mary, I can understand why you don't want to ever lose your mentor and your friend. But if you really understood what was going on, you'd realize that after I ascend, you will have me all the time and forever. The way I am right now, Mary, there is a chance you could lose me. Somebody could put you in jail, and I wouldn't be there. But if I ascend to the Father, you will have me forever. If somebody puts you in the deepest, darkest dungeon I'll be right there with you. You'll have that intimacy; you'll have that fellowship. Nothing at all will ever be able to take me away from you."

St. Augustine said it like this: "You ascended from before our eyes and we turned back grieving, only to find you in our hearts."[34] Jesus is telling Mary, "You can let go of my hand, for I can give you something better than my hand in your hand. I can put my heart in your heart."

I know this may sound sentimental. We're used to this kind of language in movies and pop songs, and so when I use it here, your mind naturally slots it into the category of romantic fiction. But what Jesus makes possible in his ascension is wholly unlike one of those scenes. He is the only one with the ability to keep his promise to be with us forever, and what he promises is beyond romantic bliss. The Bible teaches that from the throne of the universe Jesus uses his power to "raise up our affections" toward him.[35] Ephesians 2:6 says that, since Christian believers are united with Christ, in some mysterious way we are already "seated . . . in the heavenly realms" with him. At the very least this means that through the Holy Spirit our affections—the deepest desires and longings of our hearts—can be engaged with and satisfied in Christ in a powerful way.

And I do mean powerful. The great eighteenth-century pastor and theologian Jonathan Edwards wrote a "personal narrative" describing his life of prayer and meditation. He wrote,

> I very frequently used to retire into a solitary place, on the banks of Hudson's River, at some distance from the city, for contemplation on divine things. and secret converse with God; and had many sweet hours there. . . . I had then, and at other times, the greatest delight in the holy Scriptures, of any book whatsoever. Oftentimes in reading it, every word seemed to touch my heart. I felt a harmony between something in my heart, and those sweet and powerful words. I seemed often to see so much light exhibited by every sentence, and such a refreshing food communicated, that I could not get along in reading; often dwelling long on one sentence, to see the wonders contained in it, and yet almost every sentence seemed to be full of wonders. . . .[36]

Here's an account of one of the highest points in one of Edwards's times of fellowship with Christ. He says,

Once, as I rode out into the woods for my health, in 1737, having alighted from my horse in a retired place, as my manner commonly had been, to walk for divine contemplation and prayer, I had a view that for me was extraordinary, of the glory of the Son of God as mediator between God and man, and of his wonderful, grateful, pure and sweet grace and love, and meek and gentle condescension. This grace, that appeared was so calm and sweet, appeared also great above the heavens. The person of Christ appeared ineffably excellent, with excellence great enough to swallow all my thought and conception, which continued, as near I can judge, about an hour, which kept me for the greater part of the time in a flood of tears. I felt an ardency of soul to be what I know not otherwise to express, emptied and annihilated; to lie in the dust and be full of Christ alone, to love him with a holy and pure love; to trust in him, to live upon him, to serve and follow him, and to be perfectly sanctified and made pure, with a divine and heavenly purity. I have several other times had views very much of the same nature, and which have had the same effect.[37]

Now perhaps you say, "Well, I suppose there have always been a few unusual saints—special people for whom Jesus becomes that real." But that shows you don't understand the truth of the ascension. Paul speaks of the love of Christ being "poured out into our hearts" (Romans 5:5) as one of the marks of being a Christian. And, Paul says, it is because Jesus "is at the right hand of God, and is also interceding for us" (Romans 8:34) that nothing can separate us from his love. Because Christ is ascended we can know his presence, actually speaking to us, actually teaching us, actually pouring his love out into our hearts—through the Holy Spirit. His presence is not just for a select group of mystically attuned or emotionally high-strung or morally spotless saints. No: Jesus has passed into heaven, out of the space-time continuum, so that he can come into anyone's life as a living, bright reality of love and personal connection.

But the ascended Christ is not only sublimely personal; he's also supremely powerful. He controls all things for the church, and therefore you can face the world with peace in your heart. Ephesians 1, speaking of God the Father, reads: "He raised Christ from the dead and seated him at his right hand in the heavenly realms, far above all rule and authority, power and dominion and . . . placed all things under his feet and appointed him to be head over everything for the church, which is his body." Notice that little word *for*. Ephesians 1 is saying that the man who died for you is now not only at the right hand of the divine throne but he's there as the executive director of history, directing everything for the benefit of the church. If you belong to him, then everything that happens, ultimately happens for you.

The seventeenth-century Heidelberg Catechism was produced by the earliest Protestant churches in Germany to be a summary of biblical teaching, and Answer 46 says that Christ was taken up into heaven and "*he continues there for our interest*, until he comes again to judge the quick and the dead." That is simply summarizing what Paul says in Ephesians 1. Jesus' ascension was not merely a great honor for him, but it also was for us! He went to heaven to get things done for our good.

The other classic text on this attribute of Jesus is Romans 8:28 (ESV). "And we know that for those who love God all things work together for good, for those who are called according to his purpose." In this verse it is important to notice the word *together*. It keeps this out of the realm of greeting-card-style wishful thinking. Paul is not saying that every bad thing that happens to you is actually good or that every cloud has a silver lining. No, he is saying that from the vantage point of eternity, looking back on all of history, it will be clear that even the genuinely bad things that happened were incorporated and used by God—so that in the end they only accomplished the opposite of what they intended. We will see that evil things ultimately brought about more glory and good than if they had not happened. One microcosm of this is the case of Joseph's brothers, who did great evil to him and others, but in the end (as Joseph said to them), "You intended to harm me, but God intended it for good" (Genesis 50:20). Another case study is the story of Job. In the beginning of the book, Satan gets permission from God to attack Job. But in the end Satan's plot served only to produce a part of the Bible that has helped millions of people over the centuries to be faithful to God under suffering. Not what Satan intended, was it? Thus it will ever be. The ultimate case of this principle is the fate of Jesus himself, in his rejection, betrayal, torture, and death. When the forces of darkness unleashed themselves on him to destroy him, they only succeeded in vanquishing themselves (Colossians 2:15).

To say Jesus is making *everything* work together for your good means that not only are bad things part of his plan but also little things. When I was in seminary, preparing for ministry, I wasn't sure what denomination to go into. Part of the reason was that I was unsure what I believed about certain issues like baptism and predestination. During my last semester in seminary I had a professor who convinced me of the Presbyterian position on several key issues. That opened the way for me to become a Presbyterian. And that led to my eventual call to go to Manhattan to start a new congregation, Redeemer Presbyterian Church. When teaching on "God's Plan," I often like to use this as an illustration:

The reason I am in New York City today (I say to the people listening to me in the city) is because one particular teacher in seminary convinced me to go into Presbyterian ministry.

He was teaching that semester because, as a British subject, he had been granted a visa to come and teach. He had had a great deal of trouble getting that visa and had almost given up coming to the United States until someone in the State Department helped his application along. That was possible because a member of the family then in the White House was attending our seminary. That family was in the White House because the previous president had to resign. The reason he had to resign was because of the Watergate wire-tapping scandal. The Watergate scandal only came to light because a night watchman noticed an unlatched door. If that door had been latched, and the scandal had not happened, and the changes in government had not occurred, I never would have sat under that professor.

At this point I ask my hearers: "Are you glad Redeemer Church is here?" When they nod, I respond, "Then Watergate happened for you." Of course it happened for literally millions of other reasons as well. God's plans are intricate beyond our ken. But this means, in the end, that you can relax and be at peace. The man who died for you, who still has the nail prints in his hands—the signs of his suffering for you—is in control of everything at the right hand of the Father. Can you relax? Are you anxious? Are you feeling you can't keep everything going; you've got to keep all these balls up in the air? Then you don't believe in the ascension or you're not using it as a resource.

Finally, the ascended Christ guarantees that you can know you are forgiven, accepted, and delighted in by God the Father. According to the New Testament, Jesus' ascension means he is our high priest—representing us before the throne of divine justice. As Paul puts it in legal language, Jesus "intercedes" for us. This is what he promised the disciples he would do as our advocate; and the ascension allows him to keep his promise. Here's how this idea is expressed in Hebrews 7 and 1 John 2:

> [We have] such a high priest [who] truly meets our need—one who is holy, blameless, pure, set apart from sinners, exalted above the heavens. Unlike the other high priests, he does not need to offer sacrifices day after day, first for his own sins, and then for the sins of the people. He sacrificed for their sins once for all when he offered up himself. . . . Therefore he is able to save completely those who come to God through him, because he always lives to intercede for them. (Hebrews 7:26–27, 25)

> If anybody does sin, we have an advocate with the Father—Jesus Christ, the Righteous One. He is the atoning sacrifice for our sins. (1 John 2:1–2)

These metaphors—priest, advocate, intercessor—extend the mysterious but extremely important metaphor of Jesus

Christ at the right hand of the Father. Whoever is at the right hand of the throne has power to execute the royal will, but that person also has, as it were, the royal ear. And so, of course, if a person or a matter comes up before the judgment seat of the throne, there is no stronger advocate possible than the one who is at the right hand.

Remember that if you are to appear in court, everything depends on your defense lawyer, your advocate. If your advocate is brilliant, you appear brilliant. If he wins his argument, you win your case. If your advocate knows the law and is highly respected by the court, your case is secure. So when the Bible says that Jesus stands as our advocate and representative before the throne of the universe, it is a way to say that he is ascended and not just levitated. It doesn't matter who you have been or what you have done. It doesn't matter how flawed and foolish you are. When the eyes of God the Father look at you, they see the ascended Jesus; when they listen to you, they hear him. When God looks and listens to you, he sees and hears infinite beauty. In the book of Acts we are told the story of Stephen the preacher, who was put on trial for his life on trumped-up charges. As they were about to execute him by stoning, Stephen was suddenly given a vision. He says, "Look! . . . I see heaven open and the Son of Man standing at the right hand of God" (Acts 7:56). He sees Jesus not sitting at the right hand but standing on his behalf, advocating for him. It is said that Stephen had the face of an angel the whole time (Acts 6:15).

Do you know why? He understood—especially in the last moment of his life—that the one who died for him was now the ascended one who represented him before the judgment seat of the universe. He truly saw how vital that was, which meant he didn't need to care what anyone else said of him. The verdicts of earthly courts didn't matter when he knew how he was regarded by the heavenly one, the only one who mattered, in the only verdict that would last. It didn't matter whether his powerful enemies were calling him defiled, when in God's eyes he knew he was pure. Here's a man so truly self-actualized, to use a phrase once popular in the world of psychology, that he can forgive the people who are about to execute him (Acts 7:60). Why? He understood the meaning of the ascension. Do you? If you believe in him, he ever lives to intercede for you.

Do you have the kind of communication and fellowship with the ascended Christ that the Bible says is available? Do you have the peace of mind that comes from knowing your Savior controls all things for you at the right hand of the Father? Do you have the unsinkable joy and self-image that comes from understanding Christ's intercession at the right hand of God? Jesus Christ went to the right hand of the throne to be our prophet, king, and priest. He is our intimate, our leader, and our intercessor—on a cosmic scale. Do you know him in this way? If you want to live and die with the same kind of power that Stephen had, draw directly on the doctrine of the ascension.

TEN

THE COURAGE OF MARY

In this final chapter I want to consider the story of the annunciation—the angelic announcement to Mary that she would give birth to the Messiah. This account is not, strictly speaking, an event in the life of Jesus, and of course it happens prior to all the others we have examined. So why are we looking at it, and why are we looking at it last? I want to examine closely Mary's response to the message of the angel, for in some ways Mary is like us. She has not met the earthly person of Christ, and neither have we. But she receives a message about him. It is basically the gospel message, describing who Jesus is and what he will do. And Mary responds in a wonderful, moving way. In her shining example, we get crucial insights about how we should respond to all the things we have been reading about Jesus in the first nine chapters of this book.

Here is the account of the annunciation in Luke 1:

In the sixth month of Elizabeth's pregnancy, God sent the angel Gabriel to Nazareth, a town in Galilee, to a virgin pledged to be married to a man named Joseph, a descendant of David. The virgin's name was Mary. The angel went to her and said, "Greetings, you who are highly favored! The Lord is with you." Mary was greatly troubled at his words and wondered what kind of greeting this might be. But the angel said to her, "Do not be afraid, Mary; you have found favor with God. You will conceive and give birth to a son, and you are to call him Jesus. He will be great and will be called the Son of the Most High. The Lord God will give him the throne of his father David, and he will reign over Jacob's descendants forever; his kingdom will never end." "How will this be," Mary asked the angel, "since I am a virgin?" The angel answered, "The Holy Spirit will come on you, and the power of the Most High will overshadow you. So the holy one to be born will be called the Son of God. Even Elizabeth your relative is going to have a child in her old age, and she who was said to be unable to conceive is in her sixth month. For no word from God will ever fail."

"I am the Lord's servant," Mary answered. "May your word to me be fulfilled." Then the angel left her.

At that time Mary got ready and hurried to a town in the hill country of Judea, where she entered Zechariah's home and greeted Elizabeth. When Elizabeth heard Mary's greeting, the baby leaped in her womb, and Elizabeth was filled with the Holy Spirit. In a loud voice she exclaimed: "Blessed are you among women, and blessed is the child you will bear! But why am I so favored, that the mother of my Lord should come to me? As soon as the sound of your greeting reached my ears, the baby in my womb leaped for joy. Blessed is she who has believed that the Lord would fulfill his promises to her!" (Luke 1:26–45)

What do we learn from the angel about who Jesus is? The message calls him the Son of the Most High. Now, sometimes in ancient languages you could be called a son of someone if you resembled or believed strongly in that person. In John 8, Jesus has a highly charged argument with the religious leaders, who claimed to be children of Abraham and of God. Jesus countered that they were children of the devil because they lied like him! But this title means much more than that Jesus was simply a follower of God, because the angel adds, "He will reign over the house of Jacob forever." Forever? And then— perhaps because he knows that Mary can't believe her ears—he makes the same statement in another way: "His kingdom will never end." He is saying, "I really do mean *forever*." So there is a promise that this child who is about to be born will not just be a mere political king, but will have a kingdom that will last forever. Indeed, the strong implication is that he is more than a mortal human being.

And then the angel says, "The power of the Most High will overshadow you." That is a fascinating, mysterious statement, is it not? "[It] will overshadow you, so the holy one"—literally the text just says "the holy"—"to be born will be called the Son of God." Now we are being told that this supernatural, eternal being will come into the world through a miraculous birth. And he will be called *the* Son of God—not merely because his character will bear a strong resemblance to God's, but because the very divine nature of God is going to be implanted in Mary in physical form. And therefore the one to be born will be perfectly holy, absolutely sinless, and will live forever as a both divine and human person. It is an utterly astounding statement. And an elegant and concise summary of what has come to be called the doctrine of the incarnation— that God became incarnate when the Son of God assumed a human nature and was born, in the flesh, into the world.

A second thing we learn about him is that his name is Jesus, which means "God who saves." A more appropriate name could not be imagined. Every founder of every other religion comes to the world as a human being, as a guide to show us the way of salvation. None would ever claim to be God or even a redeemer or savior. But the Bible says Jesus *is* the way of salvation—living the life you should live and even dying the death you should die for your sins. So in the very name of this child we see the uniqueness of Christianity in general and of Jesus in particular. Again we see an ocean of truth put into a concise statement—into one name, actually.

And already this message makes it impossible to say that all religions are basically alike. In many circles in our society it is almost a rigid orthodoxy to insist on this. Some say all religions are equally wrong, others that they are all equally right. I completely understand the motivation for taking this position. It aims to prevent the attitude of deadly triumphalism that many religious people—including Christians—have adopted, with tragic results. But the argument that Christianity is fundamentally the same as all the rest simply will not work. On nearly every page the New Testament makes claims about Jesus that no other religion would ever make about anyone. They are so prevalent we may not even notice them.

Notice, for example, what Elizabeth says to Mary. In the last verse of the account she says Mary is blessed if she believes "what the Lord has said" to Mary when he sent the angel to speak to her. But immediately before that, she addresses Mary as "the mother of my Lord." That's amazing. How can Mary's unborn (as yet unconceived!) child be the Lord who sent her the message about the unborn child? Remember that Elizabeth is prophesying here under the power of the Holy Spirit.

It's highly unlikely she understands the meaning of all she is saying. But the implication is clear—the baby who is about to be born is the eternal Lord God who sent her the message. It is a shocking, striking claim.

Remember that the Hebrew idea of God was different from those of other cultures. When the Bible speaks of Jesus as divine, that does not mean he has more of the divine spark of life that is found in everyone. To the Hebrews, God was not an impersonal force that is part of all being but a unique, personal yet infinite, immanent yet transcendent, eternal Creator who existed before and above all other beings. To call Jesus divine while holding that understanding of divinity was stupendous. Yet it is the lynchpin of Jesus' own self-understanding and underlies everything he teaches. So you either have to say that Jesus Christ is, as the Bible claims, the unique Creator God who has come in the flesh, which makes Christianity a better revelation of God than other religions—or you have to say that he was wrong or lying, which makes him and his followers a worse revelation of God. But Christianity can't be a religion just like the rest.

Some years ago I was on a panel with a Muslim cleric, talking about our differences in front of a group of college students. And one college student kept insisting, "Well, I listened to you both for twenty minutes, and I want you to know that I just don't see any real difference between you. I just don't see any difference between the religions. It seems like they're basically saying God is love and we should love God and love one another." In our responses to the student the cleric and I were in complete agreement. At first glance it looks tolerant to say "you are both alike," but each of us argued gently that the student was not showing enough respect to listen to each religion's distinctive voice. Each faith had made unique claims that contradicted the deepest teachings of other faiths. And so, we concluded, while each faith could certainly appreciate wisdom in the other, we couldn't both be right at the deepest level. The student maintained his position, saying that all religions are fundamentally alike.

Ironically, the young man was being every bit as dogmatic, superior, and ideological as any traditional religious adherent can be. He was saying, in essence, "I have the true view of religion, and you don't. I can see that you are alike, but you can't. I am spiritually enlightened, and you aren't." But as I spoke to him a bit afterward I concluded that he was motivated by an underlying fear. If he granted that any religion made unique claims, then he would have to decide whether or not those claims were true. He did not want the responsibility of having to ponder, weigh it all, and choose. Among young secular adults it is common to adopt this belief that all religions are roughly the same. Dare I say this is a form of emotional immaturity? Life is filled with hard choices, and it is childish to think you can avoid them. It may seem to get you out of a lot of hard work, but the idea of the equivalence of religions is simply a falsehood. Every religion, even those that appear more inclusive, makes its own unique claim. But Jesus' claims are particularly unnerving, because if they are true, there is no alternative but to bow the knee to him. The annunciation pushes the exclusivity of Jesus right in our face. It demands a response and shows us there is a lot of hard work to do.

The annunciation was a shock to Mary as much for social reasons as theological ones. At the time, Mary was probably fourteen years old, and very poor. Evidence of her place on the socioeconomic scale can be seen when Mary and Joseph go to the temple to have Jesus circumcised. The offering given for the ceremony depended on the social class of the family. If you were the poorest of the poor you simply offered up two birds, and that was what the family of Jesus did. Mary is a peasant, and on top of that, she will face disgrace over this news. And yet this disgraced, pregnant, unwed peasant girl is today one of the most famous human beings in the history of the world. By contrast most of us will be forgotten in a couple of generations. What makes her great? It is how she responds to God and his message. She does four things.

The first thing Mary does is think. She uses her powers of reason. On this point we are ill-served by our translations. Right after the angel appears, the text says: "Mary was greatly troubled at his words and wondered what kind of greeting this might be" (Luke 1:29). But the word *wondered* in the verse is the word *deologistico*, which means to use logic, to reason with intensity. It means that Mary was trying to figure out how it could all be true.

This might strike us as odd. Today we like to say that we are rational and scientific people—we ask hard questions, use logic, and demand empirical evidence—and therefore it is impossible for us to believe in the appearance of an angel. The implication is that ancient people were superstitious and had no problem believing in the supernatural. We assume that if an angel showed up, people of that time simply said, "Oh, it's an angel. Hello. What's the message, please?" It's an arrogant and paternalistic view of our ancestors, not to mention a willful misreading of the text. We see here Mary struggling to understand and believe what she was hearing.

Why? Mary was Jewish. This news certainly did not fit in with what Mary knew—because the message meant a human being would be divine. The idea that the God of Mount Sinai would become human was impossible to the reason and repugnant to the moral sensibility of the Jews. (This is part of the reason why it was so difficult for Mary Magdalene and the disciples to "hear" Jesus telling them repeatedly that he would actually be resurrected.) Mary therefore had different *kinds* of rational barriers to believe the prophetic message than a modern person might have, but the ones she faced were just as big as ours. It was just as hard for Mary, in her own way, to believe the gospel as it is for us today. The annunciation was and is a major challenge to all paradigms and worldviews. There is no place in the world, and there has never been a period of history, where there are not enormous barriers to believing the proclamation that the Creator God of the universe is coming into a girl's womb to be born as a human being through her. At no time has that idea fit comfortably with the prevailing wisdom of the age. So the annunciation takes on all cultural narratives and demands hard intellectual work; and Mary does not shirk it. She does just what Jesus challenges Nathanael, the skeptical student, to do. She ponders the evidence, weighs the internal consistency of the claims, and concludes that it is true. And if she can do that, we, too, must be willing to use our reason to weigh the Christian message.

The second thing Mary does is to express her doubts openly. She says to the angel, "How will this be, since I am a virgin?" Again, Mary is not credulous. She doesn't say, "Well, you're an angel and this is all miraculous. So I'll just accept it." No, she says something any rational person would say. How can she have a child if she isn't having sex? This is an openly expressed doubt—to an angel! That shows a willingness to be honest about her uncertainties and questions. Now, I would say there are two kinds of doubts: dishonest doubts and honest doubts. Dishonest doubts are both proud and cowardly; they show disdain and laziness. A dishonest doubt is to say, "What a crazy idea!" and then just walk away. "That's impossible" (or its more contemporary version, "That's stupid") is an assertion, not an argument. It's a way of getting out of the hard work of thinking. But by contrast, honest doubts are humble, because they lead you to ask questions, not just put up a wall. And when you ask a real question, it makes you somewhat vulnerable. Mary's question to the angel actually asks for information and leaves her open to the possibility of a good answer that would cause her to shift her views. Honest doubts, then, are open to belief. If you are really asking for information and good arguments, you might get some.

And here's what I find wonderful. If she had never expressed a doubt, the angel would never have spoken one of the great statements in the Bible: "Nothing will be impossible with God" (Luke 1:37 ESV). I'm so grateful for her doubt, because that statement has been comforting and guiding me for years. All kinds of people have been helped immensely by those words. And the only reason we get this extra revelation is because Mary doubted. The more you are willing to express doubt honestly and humbly, the more you bring up your honest questions, the further you, and the people around you, are going to get. I have seen plenty of people who refuse to ask questions and refuse to express their doubts. Some refuse out of hard-heartedness, while others refuse because they think somehow it is disrespectful. Please don't dare not to raise your honest doubts and questions.

The third thing Mary does is surrender completely. Yes, eventually this does have to happen. After she hears "Nothing will be impossible with God," she makes her move. Actually,

"Nothing will be impossible with God" is a good argument. Do you believe in God, Mary? Yes. Well, if there is a God who created the world, who delivered your people and protected them for centuries, why couldn't he do this? And that made sense to her. And so Mary says, "I am the Lord's servant, may it be to me as you have said" (Luke 1:38). That is a modern translation, but I prefer the elegance of the old King James Version, which says, "Behold the handmaid of the Lord; be it unto me according to thy word."

People sometimes say to me, "I would like to be a Christian, but will I have to do this? Will I have to give up doing that? Will I have to pray, give up sex, quit my job, change my views?" Certainly, questions like this have some legitimacy, because you do need to consider what it will cost you to become a Christian. Jesus himself tells us to "count the cost" of discipleship (Luke 14:25–33). But I'm afraid many people want to negotiate the cost rather than count it. That is, they are willing to give up things, but they won't give up the right to determine what those things are. They want to be in a position to do ongoing cost-benefit analyses on various kinds of behavior, which keeps them in the driver's seat, on the throne of their life, as it were. I once heard a Bible teacher put it like this— "When it comes to following Jesus, the hardest thing to give is *in*." When God comes to Abraham, he says, "Abraham, get out of your homeland, out of the land of the Chaldees, and follow me." Abraham says, "Where am I going?" And God essentially says, "I'll show you later." God wants Abraham to give up the right to determine for himself the best way for him to live.

In some fashion you have to say what Mary said when you give your life to Christ. Your heart must say something like this: "I do not know all that you are going to ask of me, Lord. But I'll do whatever you say in your Word, whether I like it or not, and I'll accept patiently whatever you send into my life, whether I understand it or not." In other words, you simply cannot know ahead of time all the things God will be asking you to do. For example, most know that the Bible says we should not lie or cheat. But we may come to a place where telling the truth will cost us our career and telling a lie will save it. And thus following Christ will cost you dearly. So when we get to a spot like that, we must already have had it settled what we will do. You can't know the cost of following Jesus ahead of time. So you must simply say, "I do not know all that is going to come, but one thing I know—I give up the right to decide whether or not I will do God's will. I will do it unconditionally."

Mary certainly couldn't know all that it would cost, though she must have had some idea. And so, eventually, did Joseph. It is interesting to compare Luke 1 with Matthew 1. Luke 1 gives us Mary's perspective on the annunciation, while Matthew 1 gives us Joseph's. When Joseph discovered Mary was pregnant, and he knew that he was not the father, he decided to break off the engagement. But an angel appeared and gave Joseph his own message from God—he was to marry her anyway. Now, Joseph knew that if he married her, then everybody in their small town, in their shame-and-honor society, would know that the child had been conceived out of wedlock. They knew how to read a calendar. In fact, most of Mary's friends would discern she was pregnant before the wedding. Sooner or later, everyone would know that either they had sex before marriage or she was unfaithful to him, and in either case they would have violated the moral and social norms of that culture. They would forever be second-class citizens within their society. They and their children would be shunned by some, always suspected by everyone else.

So what did it mean for Joseph and Mary to accept the Word of the Lord, to say, "We embrace the call to receive this child. We will accept whatever comes with it"? What did it take for them to literally have "God with us" in their midst (Matthew 1:23)? What does it take to be *with him*? This text's answer is *courage*. And a willingness to do his will, no matter what.

When the angel said to Joseph, "Marry her," he was saying, "If Jesus comes into your life, you are going to be rejected. You will have to kiss your stellar reputation good-bye." And he married her. Surely some of Joseph's friends said, "Why in the world did you marry her? Either you did that or she was unfaithful to you." Can you imagine Joseph trying to tell them the truth? "Oh, I can explain. She is pregnant through the Holy Spirit. We learned all about it from the angels." The truth wasn't something his friends would understand, and therefore he knew they would always think ill of him.

There are many places in the world now where, if you are a professing Christian, you are going to be walking in Joseph's and Mary's shoes. For example, Christian belief sounds just as incredible and implausible to many friends in New York City as the angels' story sounded to Mary and Joseph's friends. If you are open about your Christian faith in whatever social circles or professional networks or vocational fields you are in, a lot of people just won't understand, and you won't be able to make them understand why you are the way you are. In many cases your reputation may suffer.

And yet, why do you think Jesus Christ came into this world through a pregnant, unwed teenage girl in a patriarchal shame-and-honor culture? God didn't have to do it that way. But I think it was his way of saying, "I don't do things the way the world expects, but in the opposite way altogether. My power is made perfect in weakness. My Savior-Prince will be born not into a cradle in a royal palace but into a feed trough in a stable—not to powerful and famous people but to disgraced peasants. And that is all part of the pattern. For Jesus will win salvation through weakness, suffering, and death on the cross. He will achieve power and influence through sacrificial service. And if you have Jesus in your life, you will taste much of the same treatment. But my salvation works like this—suffering leads to glory and death to resurrection. So have no fear. Receive Jesus Christ into your life, and *I* will be your honor. It doesn't matter what the world thinks."

So Mary and Joseph were willing to do for Jesus what Jesus was going to do for them. He became obedient to his Father, even unto death on a cross (Philippians 2:4–11). And when God called, they gave up their right to self-determination. If you really want Jesus in the middle of your life, you have to obey him unconditionally. You have to give up control of your life and drop your conditions. You have to give up the right to say, "I will obey you *if. . . .* I will do this *if . . .*" As soon as you say, "I will obey you *if,*" that is not obedience. What that is really saying is: "You are my consultant, not my Lord. I will be happy to take your recommendations. And I might even do some of them." No. If you want Jesus *with you*, you have to give up the right to self-determination.

Mary does one last thing that can instruct us. She goes to Elizabeth, who speaks to her in the power of the Holy Spirit. That must have helped Mary a great deal. It certainly encouraged her; and it might have helped her understand her situation in a new way. For as soon as Elizabeth is done speaking, Mary breaks into a magnificent song. Indeed, it has been called "The Magnificat." She begins to worship and adore God with all her heart: "My soul doth magnify the Lord, and my spirit doth rejoice in God my Savior" (Luke 1:46–47). In that song

Mary goes back through the Old Testament—from the Psalms and Isaiah and the prophets—making remarkable connections that reveal the coming of the divine Messiah. The annunciation is *not* a contradiction of biblical faith but is rather its fulfillment. These insights all come because she visits Elizabeth.

So the fourth thing you need is community. Mary does not appear to understand what is going on until she goes to see another believing sister, and they talk together and worship together. Yes, like Mary you need to think intensely and doubt openly, and eventually surrender completely—but it won't be enough to simply do that as a solitary individual, without trusted friends around you. Some of us don't want people to know we are even having spiritual struggles until after we have gone through them and we can tell people about them in the past tense: "That was a dark time." But in the end, you are never going to make it without community.

Mary was a nobody who became greater than everybody, simply because God came to her and she responded in the humblest possible way. She reasoned, she doubted, she surrendered, she connected with others. You can, too.

ACKNOWLEDGMENTS

I want to thank Jon Drake and the many student leaders of the Oxford Inter-Collegiate Christian Union, the organization that graciously invited me to give talks on Christianity in the Oxford Town Hall in early February 2012. That was a week in which the Christian students of the colleges of Oxford University welcomed me and my family—my wife, Kathy, and my son and daughter-in-law Michael and Sara—to be partners with them in sharing their faith and lives with their friends and colleagues. Every night after an intense couple of hours speaking to students en masse and one-to-one, my family would troop (sometimes through the snow) back through the center of Oxford and talk about the day in front of a huge seventeenth-century fireplace. I always went to bed with mingled feelings of inadequacy and joy. The first five chapters in this book are based on those evening talks.

I also want to thank Mark Campisano, who, for many years

and at great personal sacrifice, sponsored and led an early morning breakfast for businessmen at the Harvard Club in midtown Manhattan. For years I participated as a speaker. Usually the venerable, wood-paneled room was full or even overflowing, and month after month for eighteen years Mark and others around him sought to present Christianity in a familiar setting to their center city business colleagues. Over the years many subjects were touched upon, but one year I did a series of talks on the person and work of Jesus, and the last five chapters in this book were based on those messages.

Finally, this material could never have received written form without the long and skillful labors of my colleague in ministry at Redeemer City to City, Scott Kauffmann. Scott loves words, he loves theology, and he loves to imagine people's amazed faces as the wonder of the Gospel dawns on them. That makes him a great editor for me and partner in this work—the ministry of the Word through literature. Thanks, Scott.

Notes

ONE—THE SKEPTICAL STUDENT

1. This quote and the following two are from W. H. Auden, in *Modern Canterbury Pilgrims*, ed. James A. Pike (New York: A. R. Mowbray, 1956), 41. Also cited in Edward Mendelson, "Auden and God," *The New York Review of Books* 54, no. 19, December 6, 2007.

TWO—THE INSIDER AND THE OUTCAST

2. Quoted at www.bible.org/illustration/boris-becker.
3. Quoted in Alistair Begg's *The Hand of God* (Chicago: Moody, 2001), 77.
4. David Foster Wallace, commencement address at Kenyon College, May 21, 2005. Accessed at www.manic.com/sg/water.

THREE—THE GRIEVING SISTERS

5. Maybe the single best book to read that covers these points is Richard Bauckham's *Jesus: A Very Short Introduction* (Oxford, 2011). Bauckham gives a summary of the scholarship backing up each of these facts—that the Gospels are reliable eyewitness

accounts, that Jesus understood himself to be divine and claimed to be God, and that the earliest Christian church immediately worshipped him as such. In his bibliography he provides a wealth of other resources. One is his own *Jesus and the Eyewitnesses* (Eerdmans, 2006) and another is Paul Barnett, *Finding the Historical Christ* (Eerdmans, 2009).

6. See Richard Bauckham, "The Worship of Jesus in Early Christianity" in his *Jesus and the God of Israel* (Eerdmans, 2009). Also see Simon Gathercole, *The Preexistent Son of God: Recovering the Christologies of Matthew, Mark, and Luke* (Eerdmans, 2006).

7. John Gerstner, *Theology for Everyman* (Moody, 1965), 45.

FOUR—THE WEDDING PARTY

8. "John prefers the simple word 'signs': Jesus' miracles are never simply naked displays of power, still less neat conjuring tricks to impress the masses, but signs, significant displays of power that point beyond themselves to the deeper realities that could be perceived with the eyes of faith." D. A. Carson, *The Gospel According to John* (Grand Rapids, MI: Eerdmans, 1991), 175.

9. Reynolds Price, *Three Gospels* (New York: Scribner, 1996), 132.

10. Ibid., 137.

11. Fyodor Dostoyevsky, *The Brothers Karamazov* (Raleigh, NC: Hayes Barton Press, 1963), 220.

12. From the transcript of *60 Minutes*, vol. 15, no. 21, February 6, 1983. Cited in Charles Colson and Ellen S. Vaughan, *The Body* (Word, 1992), 188.

13. Though see Luke 2:41–52.

FIVE—THE FIRST CHRISTIAN

14. D. A. Carson, *The Gospel According to John* (Eerdmans, 1991), 641.

15. From "Preface to the Complete Edition of Luther's Latin Writings (1595)," in Timothy F. Lull and William R. Russell, eds, *Martin Luther's Basic Theological Writings*, 3rd edition (Fortress Press, 2012), 497.

16. Annie Dillard, *Pilgrim at Tinker Creek* (HarperCollins, 2009), 36.

SIX—THE GREAT ENEMY

17. See Romans 8:28.

18. Andrew Delbanco, *The Death of Satan: How Americans Have Lost the Sense of Evil* (Farrar, Straus and Giroux, 1995), 19.

19. J. K. Rowling, *Harry Potter and the Sorcerer's Stone* (Scholastic, 1997), 291.

20. Edith Margaret Clarkson, "We Come, O Christ, to You" (Hope Publishing, 1987).

21. See http://www.biblebb.com/files/ryle/assurance.htm.

22. See http://www.gracegems.org/Ryle/holiness5.htm.

23. C. S. Lewis, *Mere Christianity* (HarperCollins, 2001), 37–38.

SEVEN—THE TWO ADVOCATES

24. Horatio Spafford, "It Is Well with My Soul" (1873).

EIGHT—THE OBEDIENT MASTER

25. Frederick William Danker and Walter Bauer. *A Greek-English Lexicon of the New Testament and Other Early Christian Literature* 3rd ed. (Chicago: University of Chicago Press, 2001), 303.

26. Ronald K. Rittgers. *The Reformation of Suffering: Pastoral Theology and Lay Piety in Late Medieval and Early Modern Germany* (New York: Oxford USA, 2012), 47.

27. William L. Lane. *The Gospel According to Mark* (Grand Rapids, MI: Eerdmans, 1974), 516. Another theologian who believes Jesus was getting a foretaste of the divine wrath is Jonathan Edwards. See his sermon "Christ's Agony" in many forms. One place to access it is at http://www.ccel.org/ccel/edwards/sermons .agony.html.

28. Many people misunderstand this distinction and think Christ's active obedience refers to his good life and his passive obedience refers to his death. But actually the terms refer to two aspects of all his obedience. Even in his life he was beginning to pay the penalty for sin by suffering the pangs of human life that are part of the curse for sin; and even in his death he was actively loving God and us and fulfilling the positive demands of the law. See John Murray, *Redemption Accomplished and Applied* (Grand Rapids, MI: Eerdmans, 1955), 20–22.

29. See 1 Corinthians 15:45.

30. See Galatians 3:13 and Deuteronomy 21:23.

NINE—THE RIGHT HAND OF THE FATHER

31. From the hymn "Crown Him with Many Crowns" by Matthew Bridges and Godfrey Thring.
32. Louis Berkhof, *Systematic Theology* (Eerdmans, 1941), 350.
33. Ibid., 352.
34. Quoted in Philip Yancey, *The Jesus I Never Knew* (Zondervan, 2002), 228.
35. Westminster Larger Catechism, Question and Answer 53, available at www.reformed.org/documents/larger1.html.
36. Jonathan Edwards's "Personal Narrative" in *A Jonathan Edwards Reader* (Yale University Press, 2008), 289.
37. Ibid., 293.

About the Author

Timothy Keller was born and raised in Pennsylvania, and educated at Bucknell University, Gordon-Conwell Theological Seminary, and Westminster Theological Seminary. He was first a pastor in Hopewell, Virginia. In 1989 he started Redeemer Presbyterian Church, in New York City, with his wife, Kathy, and their three sons. Today, Redeemer has more than five thousand regular Sunday attendees and has helped to start more than two hundred and fifty new churches around the world. Also the author of *Walking with God through Pain and Suffering, Every Good Endeavor, The Meaning of Marriage, Generous Justice, Counterfeit Gods, The Prodigal God, Jesus the King, Center Church*, and *The Reason for God*, Timothy Keller lives in New York City with his family.

REDEEMER

The Redeemer imprint is dedicated to books that address pressing spiritual and social issues of the day in a way that speaks both to the core Christian audience and to seekers and skeptics alike. The mission for the Redeemer imprint is to bring the power of the Christian gospel to every part of life. The name comes from Redeemer Presbyterian Church in New York City, which Tim Keller started in 1989 with his wife, Kathy, and their three sons. Redeemer has begun a movement of contextualized urban ministry, thoughtful preaching, and church planting across America and throughout major world cities.